THE WASTING OF BORNEO

THE
WASTING
OF
BORNEO

DISPATCHES FROM
A VANISHING WORLD

ALEX
SHOUMATOFF

Beacon Press
Boston

BEACON PRESS
Boston, Massachusetts
www.beacon.org

Beacon Press books
are published under the auspices of
the Unitarian Universalist Association of Congregations.

20 19 18 17   8 7 6 5 4 3 2 1

This book is printed on acid-free paper that meets the uncoated paper
ANSI/NISO specifications for permanence as revised in 1992.

Text design and composition by Kim Arney

Portions of this book have appeared in different form
as features in *Vanity Fair*, *Smithsonian*, and *OnEarth* magazines.

Library of Congress Cataloging-in-Publication Data
Names: Shoumatoff, Alex, author.
Title: The wasting of Borneo : dispatches from a vanishing world /
Alex Shoumatoff.
Description: Boston : Beacon Press, [2016] | Includes
bibliographical references.
Identifiers: LCCN 2016019720 | ISBN 978-0-8070-7824-2 (hardcover : alk. paper) |
ISBN 978-0-8070-7825-9 (e-book)
Subjects: LCSH: Shoumatoff, Alex—Travel. | Shoumatoff, Alex—Travel—
Borneo. | Voyages and travels. | Human ecology. | Ethnology.
Classification: LCC G465 .S556 2016 | DDC 915.98/30443—dc23
LC record available at https://lccn.loc.gov/2016019720

To Biruté Mary Galdikas and the
orangutans and the Penan and the other
indigenous people of Borneo's rain forest:
May your struggle to save it prevail!

———————————

CONTENTS

INTRODUCTION

ON THE 19TH OF NOVEMBER, 2013, I flew from Montreal to Dubai, where I had a five-hour layover. The transit area was a fabulous bazaar of diamond-encrusted Rolexes, Gucci, Armani, all the luxury brands. Elegant veiled women with petrodollars to burn were floating around the racks and display cases. From there I flew to Kuala Lumpur and got a shuttle bus to the budget motel where we had agreed to meet. It was a stark, Hopperesque facility where nobody ever stayed for more than a night, four stories of concrete in an ocean of oil-palm trees on the way into the city that twenty-five million souls call home. "Your friend is in the courtyard," the man at the front desk told me as he handed me my plastic key, towel, and little bar of soap. I walked out to the courtyard, wondering if I was going to have any trouble recognizing him—Davie Holderness, my best childhood buddy—after fifty-five years. I had no idea what he was going to look like. But the courtyard was small and there was only one table, and only one person sitting at it, nursing a beer. A white man of my vintage, the left sleeve of his shirt slack. Davie had told me, when I'd finally tracked him down a year ago, in eastern Washington State, how he had lost his left arm fifteen years before when a snowmobile he was traveling on at high speed flipped.

"Davie! I can't believe it!" I cried to him and he got up and called out, "Panda!" (my boyhood name, inspired by my high Tatar cheekbones and slightly slanted eyes). We hugged and took a good look at each other. Sixty-seven now, he was really distinguished looking. With his wavy gray hair and a thin mustache on his long patrician face, he bore a striking resemblance to Richard Boone in *Have Gun—Will Travel*, the TV western we used to watch religiously. We sat there together, not saying anything, settling into the fact that here we were, together again after all these years. The waiter brought me a beer, and after several minutes a gusher of memories started to pour out.

Memories of Bedford Village, New York, the picturesque old New England community forty miles north of New York City, in the heart of a magnificent hardwood forest, where we had lived until the age of thirteen. The Holdernesses lived across the street, and between the ages of seven and eleven Davie and I had spent all our free time in the woods. We fished every lake, pond, river, and creek in the thirty-nine-square-mile township. Bedford in those days was crawling with frogs, snakes, turtles and in the summer was full of birdsong and the earsplitting drone of cicadas, its meadows blazing with wildflowers and swarming with butterflies. It had a riotous abundance, a fecundity and a profusion of life that has disappeared since then from most of the United States and the world. It was paradise for kids like us.

Then we graduated from eighth grade, Davie in 1959, I a year later, and went off to different boarding schools. My dad got a job in London and we moved there for six years, and by the time I got back to Bedford, at the end of the summer of 1966, Davie had dropped out of Syracuse, and then I heard he went out west and was picking apples in Oregon or maybe Washington, and I completely lost track of him. A few years ago I started wondering where he was and wanting to reconnect with him. He was one of the half-dozen most important people in my life, someone I really loved, and I didn't even know if he was still alive.

Our paths didn't cross again until last summer, when I went out to the Big Island of Hawaii to visit the Mauna Loa Observatory for a story I was doing for *Vanity Fair*—I had become a journalist, and *Vanity Fair* had been my main outlet since 1986—investigating the human hand in the extreme weather events that are happening now with increasing regularity, almost every month, somewhere in the world. The observatory has been conducting the longest measurement of atmospheric carbon anywhere, going back to 1959. Its director, John Barnes, explained that when they began, there were 200 ppm—parts per million—of carbon in the atmosphere, more than there had been in the last two hundred ✦ thousand years. Now there are 315 ppm, and we're moving out of the climatic sweet spot that has enabled our species to have had such an astonishing spurt of cultural and technological evolution, starting with the agricultural revolution in Mesopotamia ten thousand years ago. Dr. Barnes showed me how the graphs of global mean temperature (Mann's "hockey stick") and of atmospheric carbon (the Keeling Curve) both begin to rise in 1750 when the Industrial Revolution gets going, and in 1970 they both shoot up nearly vertically. "I have no political stake in this," he assured me. "I am a scientist, and the science clearly shows that anthropogenic greenhouse gases are causing this warming spike. There is no other possible explanation."

So it's us, I thought as I drove down from Mauna Loa: the burning of fossil fuels since the beginning of the Industrial Revolution. First coal, then, with the invention of the internal combustion engine, oil; our growing numbers; the ongoing assault on the world's forests, whose trees could have removed some of the carbon we are putting into the air; and what Pope Francis calls "amoral consumerism" and "the perverse relationship between the developed and developing world." What I've been writing about for forty years, ever since I saw the horrendous fires in the Amazon in 1975.

I stayed with Zoe Thorne, Davie's first cousin, who is married to a Hawaiian volcanologist and has been living on the Big Island for years. She said Davie was living in Washington State, and had his number, so I called him and we had a great reunion for an hour or so over the phone and agreed we had to see each other at the earliest opportunity. "Maybe you can join me on one of my adventures," I suggested, and Davie said, "I'd love to, Panda."

That fall I went to Borneo to meet Biruté Mary Galdikas and the orangutans she has devoted her life to for a piece about the latest discoveries of cognitive ethology—that animals have much richer mental, emotional, and moral lives than they've been given credit for. One afternoon we drove for fifty miles past nothing, to our left, but row after row of oil-palm trees going straight to a hazy low blue ridgeline maybe thirty miles in the distance. Fifteen hundred square miles of some of the oldest and most species-rich and spectacular rain forest on Earth had been totally eradicated to make room for one profitable line after another of *Elaeis guineensis*— oil-palm trees, with big clusters of oil-rich nuts—flickering past. Dr. Galdikas has hundreds of orangutans in her care center outside the town of Pangkalanbun, confiscated from loggers and pet owners, but there is almost no forest left in central Kalimantan, the southern, Indonesian two-thirds of Borneo, where she can release them. In the late eighties the deforestation rate in Borneo was the most dramatic on Earth, and it's still happening. Rain forests one hundred and thirty million years old in places, with insects, plants, and other species that haven't even been identified, are going up in smoke. The Wildlife Conservation Society is calling it the greatest destruction of biodiversity on the planet. And almost nobody in the West knows or cares, even though we are all implicated as consumers of hundreds of modern products that contain palm oil. I knew I had to come back and write about this.

By the following fall (2013) I had a book contract and an assignment from *Smithsonian Magazine*. I was going to camp in the mountainous heart of the island with some of the last Penan hunter-gatherers, whose forest is being devastated by large-scale multinational logging operations (with most of the timber going to China). Cédric Houin, a brilliantly talented thirty-five-year-old photographer and filmmaker based, like me, in Montreal, was taking the pictures. Cédric had been to the Waorani in Ecuador and visited the Kirghiz nomads of the Pamir, so I was glad *Smithsonian* agreed he was perfect for this assignment. Plus he was going to shoot video for the pilot of a free-wheeling TV docuseries we were planning to make, to be called *Suitcase on the Loose*.

I called Davie and invited him to join us, to "return to the imaginary jungle of our childhood" and camp with these gentle hunter-gatherers in the heart of Borneo, who still hunt with blowguns. He was up for it. "I gotta warn you, Davie, it's gonna be more like Paradise Lost than the Garden of Eden," I told him. "We're going to see horrible destruction by the logging, palm plantations, and hydro dams. Ninety percent of the lowland Borneo rain forest is gone."

I told him we would be in Sarawak, the largest of Malaysia's thirteen states, which takes up the northwestern corner of the island, west of the tiny but fabulously oil-rich sultanate of Brunei and the smaller Malaysian state of Sabah. "Sarawak, from what I've been reading, is the private fiefdom of its longtime chief minister, Abdul Taib Mahmud," I explained. "He controls all the action and gets a cut of everything, he grants the logging and oil-palm concessions, and he and his family have all these companies not only in Sarawak but in Canada and the United

States. According to *Forbes* his 'supposed' personal net worth is $11 billion. Now he's building all these hydro dams—fourteen for starters, and flooding out the Penan and the other indigenous people in the interior, and there are massive protests at the dam sites that we'll probably have to go to. The police are reportedly breaking heads. The government is on the lookout for foreign journalists who are trying to expose the corruption ever since two gutsy investigators with Global Witness posing as oil-palm growers caught some of Taib's family members red-handed on hidden cameras explaining what their under-the-table commission was for a three-thousand-hectare concession of rain forest. There's not a lot of freedom of expression in Sarawak. It could be dangerous."

"No problemo," Davie said. "I could use a little excitement."

Davie and I sit together in the courtyard of the motel drinking beer and it's like half a century hasn't passed, like we're just picking up where we left off. We remember so many things so clearly, it's like they happened yesterday. "You haven't changed a bit, Panda," he observes, and I tell him, "Neither have you." He has become a real gentleman, which is not surprising, given that the Holdernesses belonged to Bedford's old-line WASP gentry and that he was such a nice person as a boy, a genuinely, congenitally gentle, humble, and meek person. Now he has the relaxed, mellow voice of someone who is in a good place, at peace with the world. "I've tried to keep up with your marriages, books, and magazine articles, but there have been so many I'm sure I've missed a few," he tells me. There isn't the mischievous twinkle he has, I now remember, when he is amused. He says this in an almost apologetic way. There isn't a sarcastic bone in his body. "As for me," he continues, "I haven't done a lot international traveling. The biggest trip I ever took was when I went out west in 1967 and got a job picking apples in Washington, and I've been there ever since. I haven't been back to Bedford since my parents died fifteen years ago."

The memories and updates keep coming, but the thing that is really grabbing our attention is the miles and miles of oil-palm trees in every direction. "I had no idea this was happening," Davie says. "This is incredible. This oil must be playing a big role in our obesity epidemic. It's in everything now. Nestlé, Unilever, Procter & Gamble are probably making billions off it."

The biggest market for palm oil is India, where it has replaced artery-clogging ghee as the main cooking oil, but there are hundreds of products in America that contain it. Cookies, lipstick, dishwashing detergent, margarine, biodiesel, you name it. It's what gives chocolate bars their appetizing sheen. Otherwise they'd look like mud. The modern world can't do without it. Forty to 50 percent of household products in countries like the United States, Canada, Australia, and England contain palm oil, and 80 percent of the stuff comes from Indonesia and Malaysia. It's a $40-billion business.

"But fifty years ago we were doing fine without it," Davie says. "I can't think of anything that contained palm oil, except of course Palmolive soap. So it's a completely manufactured market, like cigarettes and Coke."

"And now it's the second-most important oil in modern postindustrial society, after petroleum," I say. "It really is incredible when you think about it." I tell him about an e-mail I just got from another of our boomer contemporaries I was back in touch with, who said, "In some ways we grew up in a golden age, but in others it's a shame to be part of such a scourge."

"*Scourge* is the word here all right," Davie says. "I don't think I've ever been in the middle of anything as depressing and unredeeming and creepy as this. And maybe in fifteen or twenty years they'll come up with something else, and all this will have been destroyed for nothing."

Both of us are jet-lagged—Davie flew west from Seattle, and it took almost as long for him to get here as it did for me, flying east—so we turn in early. Tomorrow morning we fly across the China Sea to Miri, the second-largest city in Sarawak, where we rendezvous with Cédric and the guy who is setting up our visit with the Penan, and the adventure begins.

Our little rooms are on the fourth floor, along an open walkway that looks out on the dark sea of oil palm, bristling in the moonlight, which we pause to take in. It is dead quiet out there. No riotous insect din, frog choruses, or birdsong. A sonic flatline. The biophony, which must have been glorious here, has been completely snuffed. *Biophony*, I tell Davie, is the term of Bernie Krause, a bioacoustician I met in California who spent eighteen years going around the world and recording all kinds of animal sounds, and in the last few years has been going back to the places where he did his recordings and finding them to be dead quiet. "This is a dead zone," Davie says. "Not silent spring, but silent night." Both of us shudder involuntarily in the sticky heat that sundown has not dissipated.

I rarely have nightmares, but that night I dream of some postapocalyptic time in the future, 100 to 150 years from now, when there is no natural world anymore. What is not city or other made-over human habitat has been reduced to the monoculture of a single superplant (the Bill & Melinda Gates Foundation and other heavy hitters are already working on this) that gives you everything you need and can be grown anywhere on the planet, in the Arctic or the tropics. Humans have been homogenized and digitized and genetically modified into a single global consumer culture and are spending their waking hours in virtual worlds, encased in multimedia helmets, with no connection to the animals—the superplant having done away with the need for their existence—and the genes that code for this connection, for biophilia, have been spliced out of our DNA, along with the ones for other traits that are deemed obsolete, deviant, or otherwise undesirable.

I awaken from this nightmare to the even greater nightmare of where I am, and wonder: Is this how it's going to be for my grandchildren? The sort of childhood Davie and I had, in a forest full of wildlife only an hour from a megalopolis, is no longer possible, and this is true of a lot of places. In the village in southwestern Uganda where my wife grew up in the 1970s (and where we were married in 1990), there were zebras and buffalo, impala, baboons, and grey crowned cranes within sight of her hut. That's gone too. The world my grandchildren are going to live in is going to be unrecognizable, that's for sure. But Bedford—the place that shaped Davie and me in ways that have lasted our entire lives—is, at least physically, remarkably unchanged.

PART ONE

THE EDUCATION
OF AN ANIMIST

SOME SAY THAT WE are fully formed by the time we are eight years old. I would say that definitely by the age of thirteen, I was well on the way to becoming the person I was going to be, already was that person, to a large extent, to the extent that any of us is anybody. As Einstein put it, "A large part of our attitude toward things is conditioned by opinions and emotions which we unconsciously absorb as children from our environment." For each of us, the place where we grow up becomes our inner universe, the locus of memories and dreams for the rest of our lives.

For me, and for Davie Holderness, that place was Bedford Village, New York.

My education as an animist, which I consider myself to be—if you asked me what my religion was, that's what I'd say—began there. What I mean by animism isn't anything mystical or exotic, but a way of being alive to the communications and connections that are constantly going on between all living things—human, animal, plants. The way, as kids, we were attuned with all the life in the woods, and our pets, and the people we met. In Bedford those impulses were fostered by the days we spent in the forest, by the conservation-minded landowners, and by my own family tradition of the serious study of nature, as well as daily interactions with the melting-pot society of the village. By the time I walked into my first rain forest and met my first indigenous people, I did so with an ease that no doubt sprang from having grown up in a forest that nurtured my own animistic sensibility, and in a multiethnic community where interaction with people of different cultures was a daily experience.

Our Property

If I close my eyes, I can hear the clinking of the chains on the cars and trucks going past our house on Route 22 during one of the frequent blizzards that dumped several feet of snow on northern Westchester in the 1950s. Route 22 was the Old Post Road from Manhattan to Montreal. An old milestone a hundred yards from us, in the village, right across from the movie theater, said:

TIMES SQUARE
43 MILES

It was still the main route north, and was just a hundred feet from our front door. Standing in front of which there is a photo of me, aged five, in a complete black-and-white Hopalong Cassidy outfit, taken in 1951.

Some winters there was a foot of black ice on Kinkel's Pond, on the other side of the village, and everybody would dress warm, in scarves and mittens, wool hats and snow pants, and skate on it, like a Bruegel painting, or a Norman Rockwell *tableau vivant*. "The real America, which doesn't exist anymore," my older brother, Nick, now seventy-three and living across the Hudson River, in the Catskills, was telling me the other day on the phone. "That's what we grew up in."

"We caught the tail end of a lot of things," I said to Davie at one point in the motel courtyard in Kuala Lumpur, and he said in his wonderfully calm and soothing way, "We sure did, Panda."

There are no blizzards in Bedford anymore, or black ice—they became casualties of global warming in the late seventies—and nobody has chains hanging in their garage, since the advent of positraction and four-wheel drive. I used to ski in our backyard, carving out a run that went down to the end of our property, starting out steeply over the pachysandra bed next to the house, then between the big maple tree (before it came crashing down on our kitchen, where we were having breakfast, during Hurricane Donna in 1954) and the impenetrable thicket of deodar cedar, and on behind the garage, past another smaller maple on the left, then the catalpa tree, which in summer had showy white flowers, huge leaves, and later long stringy pods, and down past the big weeping willow to the wet meadow that Pa never mowed because it became solid blue with forget-me-nots, with little black-spotted orange and gray butterflies called American coppers dancing over their delicate five-petaled blossoms.

After the war—Pa had served on a destroyer in the North Atlantic hunting for U-boats to drop depth charges on—he bought our house, a white clapboard farmhouse with a barn on three-quarters of an acre, for $14,000, and commuted to Manhattan for the next fourteen years, an hour each way, while Mom took care of us: Nicky, who was four years older, me, and my sister, Tonia, who came in 1953, and gardened and talked for hours with her lady friends, disseminating the latest gossip, and had supper ready when he came home. I can still hear Papa throwing open the front door in his trench coat and business suit and fedora and briefcase, whistling the two-note call of the chickadee, and we would come running down the stairs and hug him around the legs.

The property had been the farm of the old Dumauriac estate on the corner. The estate had been broken up during the Depression, but the castle was still inhabited, by the Westcotts. You could see its slate-tiled turrets behind a high stone wall. Pa had acquired our house from a plumber named Tolman, who had done a big job for a nursery and had been paid in beautiful ornamental trees, hence the profusion of them on our property.

The Holdernesses were across the street, in a larger colonial farmhouse with a barn in back. I probably first met Davie on the way to school, Bedford Elementary, which was on Court Street, which came up to the village at the corner of the apartment building where the movie theater was, that our house was on the other side of, separated from the apartment building by a big sloping lawn. We would cut through the Phillips' woods in back of our property and come out on Court Street at their pond, a hop, skip, and a jump from the school.

Davie remembers it was called the fire pond because the fire trucks up in the village filled up their tanks with its water, and that there were big carp of assorted colors in it, which he was never able to catch.

The Woods

After school, we sometimes stayed in the Phillips' woods until it was time for supper. Davie can still hear my mom calling us in: "Nicky, Panda, dinnertime." Davie was a quiet, gentle boy, with a special sensitivity to nature. He was always turning over rocks and logs to see if there were any snakes or wriggling salamanders or millipedes. I was more assertive, like a little Winston Churchill, my brother recalls, and on our expeditions in the woods, I was the leader, or considered myself to be, and Davie went along with it because he didn't have the alpha-male personality or neurochemistry, although he was a better fisherman. He had a sixth sense about fish and how to catch them. One time, below the mill on Beaver Dam Creek, he just stuck his spinner into a swirling riffle right in front of us, two feet away, and pulled out a ten-inch rainbow trout. In fact it must have been Davie who got me into fishing, because nobody in my family fished.

The Phillips' woods were mostly second-growth hardwoods, not even thirty years old, but in the middle of them there was an ancient maple tree that had been split by lightning. Half of its trunk was suspended by its branches parallel to the ground maybe six feet up, a scary distance to us as we jumped off it and grabbed one of the saplings that had sprouted around it and swung down to the ground. Twenty years later, I took my own two little boys to see the maple tree. "Boys, you're gonna love this," I told them. "There are these saplings you can swing down on like Tarzan." But the maple tree had disintegrated. The suspended trunk had fallen to the ground and was melting into the soil, a long, six-inch-high line of rich red earth. I was stunned. I thought the tree would still be there just like it was when I was a kid, that it would always be there. I had not yet realized how impermanent everything is, even then, in my early thirties, because nobody important in my life had died yet, and Bedford was such a stolid, conservative place.

The old WASP upper stratum who lived on bucolic pieces of land on the maze of old dirt roads were almost all Republicans, as were my parents. Their lives revolved around three institutions: St. Matthews, the lovely old Episcopalian country church; the Bedford Golf and Tennis Club, which Jews couldn't get into; and Rippowam, the private school, named for a long-gone local Indian chief. Some wag called them the Holy Trinity. The whole idea of the postwar suburban utopia was to insulate your children from the horrors you had known. If you played it straight and sucked it in and were active in the community, and educated your kids properly, it could go on forever. This was the theory of the golden Eisenhower years. But it only lasted until 1959. Then it all came apart in the sixties, for the Shoumatoffs, the Holdernesses, and many other dutiful, undeserving Bedford families. John Cheever, who lived over in Ossining, several exurbs west, was already exposing the dark side of the utopia in his short stories. His last book was a novel called *Oh What a Paradise It Seems*. But for Davie and me, it *was* paradise. There is no greater gift a child can be given than to have a forest to roam around in, plus we were also on the edge of the village, where there was a wonderful cast of characters, a multiethnic microcosm of the American dream, to interact with, which we were part of. A more glorious Huck and Tom childhood could not have been asked for.

Sometimes I would go into the Phillips' woods alone or with our dogs, Basta and Capri (a chocolate-colored Lab-hound mix and a light taupe Weimaraner named by my mom after we went to Italy one summer and she fell in love with all things Italian), and poke around by myself. One time I sat down on a log and just stayed still, listening and looking. Three chickadees mustered the courage, in several bursts of flight, punctuated with nervous, curious chatter, to land on the branch right above me. Suddenly everything became radiant, flooded with light. All at once, I felt this kinship with everything around me, not only the chickadees but everything I could not hear pulsing, quaking, cheeping, and singing. I was them and they were me. There was no difference between us. The chickadees piped down and we just sat there together and enjoyed the moment.

I had a number of these St. Francis experiences, but didn't tell anyone about them. My schoolmates would have laughed at me, except Davie. He would have understood, but I never told him about them either. I didn't have to. He was deliriously happy being in the woods. "It's what I lived for," he tells me now in Kuala Lumpur. And there were a number of my parents' friends who would have been delighted by a child's account of such an experience. Maybe I never told anybody because I didn't realize I had a religious experience. I didn't see it that way. I was just rapturously happy, my senses were fully open and engaged in the woods. Only in the 1970s and '80s, when I started spending time with animists like the Navajo and the Yanomami in the Brazilian Amazon, did I realize that these joyous feelings of identification with all life are perfectly normal responses to communications going on between trees, insects, mammals, birds, people, frogs, even fungi, all the time on many levels: vocal, visual, body language, olfactory, infrasound, mirror neuron, spindle cell, even quantum. If such states of heightened conscious have little currency in the modern material culture, it's because most of us are living in cities and spend our waking hours indoors, in cars and subways and commuter trains, in the virtual worlds of screens and TV and video games, and we've lost the connections that most of the people who have ever lived, the nameless thirty-eight billion hunter-gatherers who have come and gone before and since the agricultural revolution, had on a constant daily basis with their fellow-beings and devised complex mythologies and cosmologies to explain.

Experiences like mine, such animistic flashes, are common for kids in every culture who have the opportunity to be alone in nature. Paul Shepard writes, in his book *Nature and Madness*, how children's play going back to the Stone Age has always been about

> imitating, starting with simple fleeing and chasing, going on to mimic joyfully the important birds, being them for a moment and then not being them. Feeling as this one might feel and then that one, all tried on the self. The child sees the adults dancing the animal movements and does it too. Music itself has been there all the time, from his mother's song to the melodies of birds and the howl of wolves. The child already feeling the mystery of kinship: likeness but difference. Animals have a magnetic attraction for a child, for each in its way seems to embody some impulse, reaction, movement that is "like me."

Gerald Durrell's enchanting memoir of growing up on Corfu, *My Family and Other Animals*, also celebrates the child's innate attraction to and insatiable curiosity about other living things. Erich Fromm coined the term *biophilia* to describe the psychological orientation of being attracted to all that is alive and vital, and Edmund Wilson defined it as referring to "the connections that human beings subconsciously seek with the rest of life."

On the other side of the village there was an abandoned road, overgrown with brambles, that went between Mrs. Colgate's and Captain Woods's imposing Victorian mansions to the Mianus River, which it crossed in an old narrow curved stone bridge. Below the bridge the river spilled into a large pool where there were always fish, so Davie and I went there a lot. One time at the height of summer we caught a couple of yellow perch and spit-roasted them over a fire we started in the woods on the other side of the bridge. The temperature was in the nineties, and all the broad leaves on the trees and understory shrubs were dripping with moisture, and the grating din of the cicadas was like a buzzsaw cutting into steel. It was just like being in a rain forest. When I entered my first one, in Jamaica in 1970, the feeling was not at all unfamiliar, except for the bewildering diversity of unfamiliar plant species.

Davie opened his pocketknife and dug into a rotting log, where he discovered some white grubs working a seam of it. "I hear the Indians eat these things and they're delicious," he said. So we roasted them over the flames and they were, crunchy and scrumptious. Davie and I at that moment were no different from any kids who live in a forest. We could have been Indians, Pygmies, hunter-gatherers in Borneo. Children are the same in any culture, until it begins to indoctrinate them. The curiosity, the intelligence are the same at what the expressionist Willem de Kooning (I think it was he) called "the magic age between the age of four and eight, when the imagination runs wild," which he was always trying to get back to. Kids learn, like animals, being animals, by playing, and if they have a forest to explore, or a seashore, they will be endlessly fascinated by all the other forms of life and will make all sorts of new friends and connections.

The Village

When Davie and I stepped out of our houses, we had two choices: the woods or the village. The woods was the richest temperate broad-leaved hardwood forest on the planet, with forty-five hundred species of higher plants, from ferns on up then, which Bedford was in the heart of.

There was always something happening in the village. It was like William Saroyan's *The Human Comedy*, which I would read in the ninth grade. I never asked my dad why he chose to buy a house on the edge of the village, right on busy Route 22, when he could have picked one with more land on one of the quiet dirt roads, which, given his passion for natural history, would have seemed a more obvious choice. Whatever his thinking was, it enriched our lives immeasurably.

Usually when Davie and I went down to the village we were headed for Trela's, the ramshackle general store that belonged to Al Trela, our neighbor Mr. Trela's son. Trela's was crammed to the gills and overflowing with everything a kid could possibly need. Model airplanes, toy soldiers and tanks and jeeps, fishing lures, caps and cap pistols, BB guns and BBs, Lionel trains and tracks, packages of postage stamps for young collectors (I eventually acquired the Third Reich's entire series with the face of Hitler in various denominations and tints, and the bare-breasted Senegalese woman series from French Equatorial Africa). My stamp collection, learning that there were so many different countries with different people and cultures and animals as I pasted their perforated images into my album, nurtured a growing fascination with the world beyond Bedford, which I was already soaking up on our annual family summer trips to Europe, beginning when I was four.

And so Davie and I acquired, naturally, by osmosis, the accident of birth having placed us in this exurban paradise, a holistic, inclusive, ecological, egalitarian worldview in which we did not differentiate between man and nature, the village and the woods, or our own little consciousnesses wandering in them. This would influence my philosophy and approach as a conservationist, my way of writing, my whole outlook. My view of nature is more Shakespearean than Thoreauvian. It includes man and his works, however wondrous or, as I would experience when I became a journalist and started to see the treachery and violence humans are capable of, vile. It is all "nature"—what is out there, the material world. The only world, neither Davie or I doubted for a second.

The distinction between wilderness and human habitat is, of course, important for the protection of ecosystems and their native flora and fauna. The old WASP gentry, who lived in understated elegance out on the dirt roads, had a sense of stewardship toward the natural world that came with being hereditary landowners. They lived on at least four acres. There were several dozen large estates in Bedford, with hundreds of acres and columned brick mansions on their hilltops built by people who had prospered in the late nineteenth century, like the Sloanes of the Fifth Avenue department store, who had their own peacocks and grass tennis court. Every time a ball smacked the tape of the net the peacocks squawked so loud it could be heard in the valley below. None of these estates had walls and surveillance cameras like they do now. Their chatelaines, and indeed most of the women in Bedford's upper-middle class, took great pride in their gardens. In fact, the first chapter of the Garden Club of America was started in Bedford in 1938, as well as the first chapter of the National Audubon Society in 1913, and the Nature Conservancy, now a worldwide wilderness-protection operation, began with the acquisition in 1951 of the virgin hemlocks in Mianus River Gorge, just north of Bedford's border with Greenwich, Connecticut. There were a number of private nature sanctuaries in town, donated by hilltoppers, as the people with the estates were called, who didn't want to pay taxes on so many acres and didn't want to be encroached on by the hoi polloi, or simply loved their land and didn't want it to be developed and turned into suburbia. Bedford had four-acre zoning, unlike the towns to the south like Chappaqua and Pleasantville, where the houses were on much smaller lots and newer and something you'd rather die than have to live in, if you were from Bedford. This zoning was not egalitarian. Developers to the south and crusading socially conscious lawyers trying to bust it called it exclusionary, but because of it Bedford still retained much of its original rural character.

The roads in the most desirable districts were still dirt, the old country lanes from farming days, which there were still vestiges of: barns, open meadows, and pastures. Some of the houses and gravestones dated to the seventeenth century. Old stone walls ran through the woods, which were almost completely cleared for pasture by the turn of the twentieth century and began to return after cars replaced horses as the way to get around and it was no longer necessary to grow hay. The transition was pretty much accomplished by 1918, so a lot of the woods were second growth and only thirty years old—about as long as our family had been in America. But there were many magnificent old trees that had never been cut: oaks—including the five-hundred-year-old Bedford Oak, less than a mile up Route 22, on the corner of Hook Road, a symbol of the community's continuity, some of whose lateral branches are as long as it is tall and have had to be propped up—massive hickories, ashes, maples, walnut and tulip trees, red, black, white, chestnut, and pin oaks, hemlocks and white pines. The chestnut trees that had been the dominant species with the oaks now only made it to saplings before they were smitten by the blight that had come from Asia in the twenties, and the elms were succumbing to Dutch elm disease, but it was still a vibrant, powerful forest, awesome and in places cathedral-like to little kids like Davie and me. Plus there were all kinds of interesting plants that had escaped from people's gardens: winged euonymus, Japanese bamboo, rhododendrons, and lilies.

In some of the caves in the woods my older brother, Nick, found arrowheads and shreds of beaded deerskin moccasin, and ceilings still black with the smoke of three-hundred-year-old campfires lit by the Munsee Delaware, most of whom were massacred by the Dutch in 1688 and the rest deported to a series of reservations in the ever-expanding West, eventually ending up in Oklahoma. Only their place names, now stops on the Harlem Railroad line—Katonah, Mahopac, Kisco, Chappaqua—survived. Aspetong, a lake a mile from where Davie and I lived, our favorite place to fish because it had big pickerel, meant "the highest place around," because there was a hill nearby from which you could see in every direction.

Aunt Helen

One of the largest private properties in Bedford was the thousand-acre Westmoreland Farm. It belonged to Helen Clay Frick, the maiden daughter of the Pittsburgh coke baron and art collector Henry Clay Frick. Aunt Helen, as we called her, was a close friend of my grandmother and her brother, Andrey Avinoff, who had been the director of the Carnegie Museum of Natural History in Pittsburgh for twenty-five years, until three years before his death in 1948. It was she who had persuaded my parents to settle in Bedford after the war. Aunt Helen lived in the utmost simplicity in an old farmhouse, of which a lovely primitive by Grandma Moses, everything buried in snow, hung in the foyer. Below the farmhouse was a working farm that was technologically pre–World War I. The extensive flower and vegetable gardens were plowed by a workhorse named Roman Nose and the milk came from the teats of a cow named Buttercup. A little further into the property, behind a moss-covered slab dam with maiden hair ferns growing in its cracks, was a pond with a rowboat in which Davie and I would paddle to a small island that was dripping with water snakes, dozens of them sunning on the branches of its bushes hanging out over the water. The pond was shallow and slimy and full of big bullfrog pollywogs but no fish of interest, so Davie wouldn't come with me to Aunt Helen's very often. He remembers that the golden apples in her orchard were delicious.

Aunt Helen and my father bonded through their love of nature and the simplicity and austerity of their lifestyles, and we were almost like family. At Christmas she would give me a beautiful coffee-table book, about birds of the world when I was making watercolors of birds, about Florence when we had been there that summer. At the end of the fifties Pa was instrumental in her creation of the Westmoreland Sanctuary from half of her farm. He designed the cozy house for the resident naturalist and the nature museum, from the Methodist Church outside the village that was taken down and reassembled board by board, and he then served as the sanctuary's first president. Back in the woods there was a beautiful lake that became known as Bechtel Lake. The Bechtels were major benefactors of the sanctuary. They lived on Succabone Road (where Glenn Close lives now) and had a labyrinth rose garden that I loved to wander in and find my way out of.

Pa was, like Davie, a genuinely humble and self-effacing person, a real gentleman, almost obsequiously attentive to guests and never putting himself first, but he was extremely knowledgeable, particularly about natural history. He was the president of the Bedford Audubon Society, a post that my brother would take over in the seventies, with me as secretary. We always took part in the Audubon Society's annual Christmas bird count in December, freezing as it was. One time when I was four Pa took us all on a field trip to the Hudson, to a part of the shoreline where the Indians had camped long ago and where there might be some artifacts. Nobody found anything except me, who had been left playing on the rocky beach. There among the water-smoothed boulders I picked up a long grooved net sinker. The find made the local paper.

Papa was also the president of the New York Entomological Society, which met once a month at the American Museum of Natural History's Department of Entomology. Sometimes he took me with him. The society met in a room behind the scenes, behind the public displays, where the vast majority of the butterflies were, in glass cases that slid out from wooden cabinets. Pa pulled out one drawer of fantastic tropical butterflies, the famous Rajah Brooke birdwing from Borneo (Davie and I were hoping to soon be seeing some live ones), the numerous incandescent blue morphos of the Amazon. In another drawer, he showed me the by now rather ratty type specimens of Shoumatoff's hairstreak, *Nesiostrymon celida shoumatoffi,* classified by Comstock and Huntington and named by them for my father, who had caught the first specimens known to science in Jamaica in 1934, when he was sixteen (and in the late nineties elevated by Johnson to species status, *N. shoumatoffi*). In the thirties, he and his uncle had taken six trips to Jamaica and made the definitive collection of the island's butterflies and moths.

The Butterflies of Bedford

So it was only natural that I became interested in butterflies. The best place to catch them was the old Jewish golf course, a fifteen-minute walk from our house up Cross River Road, which split off Route 22 at the corner where the Westcotts lived. It had been abandoned in the thirties and was covered with all kinds of flowering plants for them to take nectar from and to feed on as caterpillars. Its overgrown fairways, like all the splendid gardens of Bedford in the summertime, were swarming with butterflies. There were several species of swallowtail in town. The tiger swallowtail was abundant, and the dark-morph female was common. Spicebush swallowtails were also abundant, the woods being full of the shrub. The pipevine swallowtail was less common, and the smaller black swallowtail was least common. It was always a special treat to see one. Monarchs were plentiful, with milkweed all over the place, as were their nontoxic mimic, the viceroy. There were five species of fritillary, red-spotted purples, white admirals, Hunter's butterflies. The rarest butterfly in Bedford was the tawny emperor. I only saw a couple and managed to catch one, sitting on a rhododendron leaf in the Moss's driveway.

I was especially on the lookout for Baltimore checkerspots after meeting Alexander Klots at one of the New York Entomological Society's monthly meetings.

Klots was writing the field guide to the butterflies of North America for the newly launched Houghton Mifflin series. He specialized in checkerspots, small, intricately mottled brown, orange, and white butterflies whose favorite food plant is turtlehead. He showed me a photo of its creamy white blossoms, which were shaped like the heads of turtle hatchlings. "I bet there are a lot of Baltimore checkerspots in Bedford," he said, "and I'll give you five dollars for every one you catch for me." This was big bucks. Think of all the stamps I could buy at Trela's! I caught a dozen on the old Jewish golf course, hovering around turtleheads they had eaten as caterpillars, and presented them to Dr. Klots in triangles of folded paper with my name and the date and place of capture written on them.

Back home I mounted the butterflies I caught and made watercolors of them with a Series 7 sable brush and tubes of Winsor & Newton watercolors with marvelous names like alizarin crimson and cadmium yellow, on smooth Whatman paper boards, which my grandmother, a professional portrait painter, gave me. My butterflies were about one-twentieth as good as her brother Andrey's, which our house was full of. I only did one, of an orange sulfur, that was halfway decent. I tried to get my wings as luminous as his by layering colors straight from the tubes with hardly any water, but they came out opaque and muddy. But looking closely at and appreciating the intricate design and palette of a butterfly's wings or a flower's blossoms had its own effect that made it worth the effort. It trained my eye and increased my awe of the creation. When you have to paint something, you have to come to terms with it—its shape, color, movement—much more intimately than if you just take a picture of it. Children see a lot of little things adults miss. They see in great detail, with a hyperspecificity more like that of animals.

The Young Mountaineer

In the late fifties my parents, after several trips to Europe, fell in love with Switzerland, specifically the Bernese Oberland and its snow peaks and glaciers and high meadows full of flowers and butterflies, and alpine environments became their ruling passion for the rest of their lives. We started to go the Alps every summer, renting a chalet first in Gstaad, then Gsteig, Kandersteg, Villars-sur-Ollon. I became, at eleven, the youngest person to climb the Mönch, the triangular snow peak between the Jungfrau and the Eiger, and dreamed of becoming a mountain guide and a fearless rock climber like Walter Bonatti. And when we were in Bedford, rather than go fishing with Davie, I would go climb and rappel down the cliffs of Indian Hill, on the way to Pound Ridge, with another kid named Roger Austin. I had a manila rope that I bought at Sharlach's, the hardware store in the village, and a brace of pitons and carabiners.

During the part of the summer when we were in Bedford, I would walk over to the Club, where I'd usually find Davie sitting around the pool. He didn't play tennis or golf and he wasn't on the swimming team. "I was much more interested in going down to the pond on the tenth hole [whose tee was next to the pool] and catching painted turtles," he says. "I spent a lot of the first half of the sixties sitting around the Club pool, waiting for something to happen. I don't know where you were during those years."

"In London, and climbing mountains in Switzerland, and one summer, when I was sixteen, my brother and I bummed around Greece," I tell him.

We figure that the period when we were inseparable lasted from third to fifth grade. It spanned the last year or so of de Kooning's magic age to the end of boyhood and the onset of pubescence at the age of eleven. I tell Davie I was just reading a profile of James Damon, CEO of J. P. Morgan Chase & Co., and he said he thinks he was fully formed by the time he was eight. "I think we were, too, Panda," Davie says. "The rest of my life has kind of been an anticlimax."

"I was in Bedford last year," I tell him, "and it was unchanged, still exceptionally beautiful. But the abundance of frogs, snakes, fish, butterflies, is gone, like everywhere. There's a new metastudy by the World Wildlife Fund that finds half the individual animals that were alive on the planet in 1970 have been killed. This summer I flew over the Alps on the way to a literary conference in Lake Como, and the snow is gone, the big peaks and the glaciers below them are just bare black rock and scree. Bedford's magnificent forest is under assault by new introduced exotic beetles and fungi, which are attacking the beeches, oaks, ashes, hemlocks, spruces, and cherry trees. You don't get the full orchestra of bullfrogs, katydids, cicadas, birds singing their hearts out at the height of summer anymore. There's been a dramatic die-off even in a place as conservation-minded and pesticide-free as Bedford. The hardest hit are the freshwater clams, which are really mussels," I go on. "They're only found in the Northeast. Thirty percent of the species are extinct. Did you know they can live to be one hundred and fifty years old?"

"No kidding, Panda," he says. "Who would have known? All I remember is they're no good to eat. I remember there were some in Aspetong Lake and we boiled them up in a pot and they tasted awful."

We fall silent, until Davie says, with a touch of sadness, "So the Eden of our childhood is still there, but the living things that made it so wonderful are pretty much gone."

Our Pets

We talk about the importance of our pets, how we already knew that Descartes's contention that only humans are capable of reason, morality, and emotions was a crock even though we had never heard of Descartes. Sometimes I slept with Basta and Capri on the living room rug. I never had the sense that there was any real difference between us. Sometimes they would yip excitedly in their sleep, so don't tell me they were incapable of dreaming and self-awareness and didn't have imaginations. Sometimes they knew when I was going to head down to the village before I did and would run excitedly to the front door, and we would go together. Wherever I was going, the village or the woods, they were up for it. Thomas, our regal Persian cat, was attuned to things that the dogs weren't. One summer we entered him in a pet show ten miles away, and he escaped from his cage. Six months later, after what must have been an incredible odyssey, he found his way back to us. And when he got old, he simply went off somewhere and died. We looked all over, but never found his body. None of the recent findings of cognitive ethology about the moral and emotional lives and intelligence of animals are at all surprising. Of course animals care: for their young—as I saw when Basta had a litter fathered by Rusty, a bloodhound who lived on Court Street—and for us. "Our dogs' love and devotion were total and unconditional," I say, and Davie says, "Like our Labs.'"

I ask him if he ever had the sort of ecstatic feeling of oneness with everything in the forest that I did a couple of times, and he says no, he never did, but he felt alive in the forest, more alive than he did anywhere. I still get that feeling whenever I walk into a forest. "People say I have shamanic qualities," I tell him, "but you were the one who was always turning over rocks and logs to see what was under them. I do, though, have an unusually responsive and inclusive biophilia. Animals, people, landscapes, forests, I love them all. I was probably born that way, but growing up in a family of natural scientists and with all the natural and human diversity in the woods and Bedford Village also nurtured it.

"The other day I asked my wife, who has a master's in clinical psychology, what syndromes did she think I have, after living with me since 1988 and knowing me better than anybody, and she said, 'Well, you're bipolar, borderline, ADD, drug-damaged, narcissistic, and obsessive-compulsive, but none of them full blown.' All of these things are definitely describing traits I have only recently come to realize I have, but they have had both positive and negative effects in my life, so I would propose a less judgmental and reductive term: *borderless personality*. When I walk into a forest, any wild place, things become alive. The usual barriers with animals and people from other cultures for me do not exist. I have kind of learned on the job, after getting down with so many animals and indigenous people who regard them as their brothers. But this does not mean I have the kind of empathy that can feel the way an animal or another person feels. I have only met a few people who have that, and you're one of them, Davie."

PART TWO

WONDER WANDERING

IN THE FALL OF 1970 I drove across the country with my dog, Willie, a collie-shepherd mix I'd picked up at the pound who was so smart and attuned to everything that was going on that a more invaluable and stimulating companion, a tighter bond, couldn't have been asked for. It was my first trip across the country. I was more traveled in Europe and Greece, and had spent a summer working construction in Alaska, living off the salmon running up the river where I had pitched my tent, so many thousands you could almost have run across it on their backs. That was an unforgettable experience: a wilderness still crawling with wildlife, spruce trees sagging with plump spruce grouse, a bear or a moose around every bend. But I had barely dipped my foot into the wonders of the contiguous United States.

In the middle of the Arizona desert I turned off the interstate onto an enticing dirt track that went into the territory of the Mescalero Apaches, and after several miles I came upon a long-haired member of the tribe who was about my age—twenty-three—sitting on a rock, alone and far from anybody or anything human. He was looking out over the desert and didn't respond, or even acknowledge my existence when I asked if he wanted a lift. He must have been on a vision quest I later realized. Traditionally, among Ojibway, or Anishinaabe people of western Canada, when you were in your early twenties, you went off "wonder wandering" for several years before settling down and raising a family. This is kind of what I was doing and am still doing, forty-seven years later. I have never stopped wandering and wondering. I was born to travel. It's in my blood, going back to a famous polar explorer in the nineteenth century and his grandson, Andrey Avinoff, my great-uncle, who was one of the first foreigners to enter Tibet, in 1912. He was look-ing for new species of *Parnassius*, the tailless gauzy-white alpine *Papilios*. From an early age I exhibited an urge to hit the road. When I was four and we were visiting my maternal grandmother at the little red farm-house in Richmond, New Hampshire, where she summered, I just took off. When my frantic mother found me, several miles down the road—I can still smell the golden floor of the needles below the tall white pines that lined it, and the tar bubbling out of the seams in the highway in the hot August sun—I was holding forth to half a dozen adults about how I was going to travel around the world and was going to be gone for two or three years. According to Mom, they were spellbound.

At this point I had shoulder-length hair myself and in keeping with the times—if I hadn't come of age in the late sixties, my life would have turned out very differently—had dropped out and been living deep in the New Hampshire woods for the last nine months. There, as my mother put it, "nature hit me." Particularly the birds, which I was painting watercolors of. I was keeping a journal of the fauna and flora I encountered and writing songs, about one a day, with lyrics full of nature imagery. My heart was bleeding for the beauty of universe. After several ecstatic trips on organic mescaline that put me in the rapturous state of oneness with all life that I had experienced as a kid in the woods in Bedford, every pore of my senses was open. But my "old lady" (as significant others were called in the hippie countercul-ture; she was a year older than me) and I broke up, and I was heading out to California, where there were two girls I wanted to be with who, when I got there, both turned out to be with other guys. I was still looking for my soul mate, who I believed was somewhere out there, and trying out different possibilities for what I was going to do with my life. I was now a singer-songwriter and a bird painter. I had given up being a newspaper reporter and trying to be the next T. S. Eliot, but I knew from the age of sixteen that I was going to be a writer. Not of fiction—truth is stranger than fiction any day of the week, it has more strange, improbable twists than the most imaginative novelist could possibly invent, and more verisimilitude, obviously. And coming from a family of natural scientists, I had too much respect for the way things are and trying to figure out the incredible intricacy of what was out there, and how everything fit and interacted, and the role of accident, to put out a narrative that cut corners. I was much taken with the new journalism of Tom Wolfe, especially *The Electric Kool-Aid Acid Test*, and with the gonzo journalism of Hunter S. Thompson's *Fear and Loathing in Las Vegas*, but they didn't give any ink to other species or the natural world, a major shortcoming. Why couldn't you write about people and animals, let them all have a voice, and convey the endless fascination of what is actually out there, if you bother to look, which not many people do? So I would open their eyes then. This is the kind of writing I was beginning to see I was put here to do. Something that incorporated my love of people, nature, and world travel.

First Encounters with Environmental Horror

I started hanging out at Wheeler's Ranch, an open commune on a spectacular ridge that ran down to the sparkling Pacific, above a funky hamlet called Occidental, an hour and a half north of San Francisco. I did a lot of jamming around the nightly bonfire with other guitar pickers, some of them drifters like me, but the sixties were over; the Age of Aquarius was acquiring a dark edge. Somebody OD'd and was found dead in the underbrush when I was there, and nobody even knew who he was.

One afternoon word came that there had been a big oil spill in San Francisco Bay; thousands of waterbirds were coated in oil and volunteers were needed to clean them off. So we all piled into our rigs and drove down to the bird collection station where we worked through the night and all next day wiping oil off the bodies and tails and feet and necks and heads of western grebes and terns, mainly, with paper towels soaked in baby oil, and daubing their eyes, ears, and nostrils out with Q-tips. The birds were in terrified shock. Some of them died in our hands. This was my first lesson in, my first harrowing actual experience of, the death and destruction that the modern, carbon-fueled way of life is wreaking on the planet, the cost of the amenities and products we take for granted. It was transformative, eye opening.

In the fall of 1971, back east, I fell madly in love with Jane Frick, Aunt Helen's great-niece, with whom I use to run around in the beautiful woods of Westmoreland Farm. She was a real nature girl who had grown up more with animals than people and had a remarkable ability to connect with them and feel what they were feeling, more than anybody I had ever met. She had become a marine biologist and an expert on green sea turtles and right and humpback whales and was working with Roger and Katy Payne, who were making the first recordings of haunting, ethereal, unfathomably complex whale songs.

That February Jane and I went together to Jamaica, my first trip to the tropics. We climbed Blue Mountain Peak and visited the Maroons, the descendants of slaves who escaped into the impenetrable Cockpit Country in the west-central part of the island and had their own treaty with the British crown. We looked for the Shoumatoff's hairstreak, the little metallic-blue lycenid named for my dad, who had caught the first specimens known to science near Accompong, the Maroon's main community, in 1934, when he was sixteen, but the only ones we found were the pinned dead ones he and Uncle (as our great-uncle Avinoff was known in the family) had deposited in the Jamaica Institute in Kingston.

We rented a bungalow in a little place west and inland from Ocho Rios called Bamboo. The bungalow belonged to Reynolds Metals. Behind it was a verdant rain forest, full of beautiful little birds found only on Jamaica, emerald-green todies and swallow-tailed hummingbirds, which Jamaicans call the doctor bird. Behind the rain forest were two hills that had been literally decapitated, cut off at the neck, and were oozing red earth like blood from a severed artery. Reynolds Metals had mined them for their bauxite and left them like that. This was my second lesson in the terrible cost of the modern way of life. Since then I avoid having anything to do with aluminum, as much as possible. A few years later I was climbing up an arroyo in the desert outside of Moab, Utah, and came upon some coyote scat. Half of it was fur and bones, but the rest was aluminum foil from some previous hiker's candy or sandwich wrapper. The sight gave me a shudder as if I had bitten into the foil myself.

I had sublet a place on the Lower East Side, a block from the Hell's Angels headquarters on Second and Second, and was supporting myself by writing articles for *Rolling Stone* and the *Village Voice* and going up to Bedford and doing tree work for my mom's friends, and with the thousand dollars I had gotten for a two-year option on the songs I had written from the manager of Muddy Waters, Joni Mitchell, and Joan Baez. I was still planning to follow in the footsteps of Bob Dylan. But then I scored a contract with Harper & Row for what would become my first book, *Florida Ramble*, about traveling around the Sunshine State in an old convertible with Willie, poking around in the swamps and talking to the crackers, retirees, fruit tramps, and so forth. Jane and I broke up, and I got involved with my editor's adorable assistant, Leslie, and we decided to get married and live in Bedford. My brother was living up in Cross River with his English wife and curating the little stone nature museum at the 4,315-acre Ward Pound Ridge Reservation, the largest park in Westchester County. Despite the museum being only one room with a bunch of stuffed animals, Nick was doing amazing things, inspiring a whole generation of kids and their parents, turning them on to the rich natural and human history of where they were. He became an expert on the Lenape Delaware who had lived in Westchester, learned their dialect, Munsee, their ethnobotany, and everything else he could about them from old ethnographies and archaeological digs. In one family's backyard he found a bear petroglyph, carved by the Lenape centuries ago on a big boulder, a glacial erratic. He made a big mandala that took up a wall of the museum and marked along its outer ring scores of local natural events over the course of a year: when the bears came out of hibernation, when the warblers returned, when the wildflowers bloomed, dozens of them, when the oaks were heavy with acorns; then in the next ring the Indians' seasonal hunting and gathering and planting activities, also very numerous and coinciding with the natural events; then in the next ring the farmer's seasonal activities, fewer but still geared to the seasons, and finally in the center, suburban man, who shoveled snow in the winter, cut the grass over the summer, and raked the leaves in the fall, and that was about it.

I got hired as the resident naturalist at the Marsh Sanctuary, a wildlife preserve on the edge of Mount Kisco, five hundred yards from the hospital where I was born. It came with a cottage, where Leslie and I lived, before and after our marriage. On one of my Sunday morning bird walks we saw the first red-bellied woodpecker ever reported in Westchester, the latest of a succession of species, following the tufted titmouse, the Carolina wren, and the turkey vulture, that were moving up from the south because of what is now recognized as anthropogenic climate change. But at that point only a handful of climate scientists knew about the greenhouse effect from CO_2 emissions accumulating in the atmosphere. When I asked a paleometeorologist at Columbia's Lamont-Doherty Earth Observatory why these southern birds were suddenly appearing, he said it was due to the interglacial warming period since the last glaciation going on longer than expected. It was overdue to end, and when it did we were going to be plunged into another ice age. This scenario, "Another Ice Age?" even made the cover of *Time* magazine in 1974.

Harper & Row signed me up for a second book, a cultural and natural history of Westchester County, and I got a job teaching middle school science at Rippowam. Many of my old beloved teachers were still on the faculty. I was supposed to teach a canned science course doing chemistry experiments and dissecting frogs, but I decided instead to teach the kids basic literacy in the local flora and fauna. My fifth and sixth graders learned to recognize thirty-nine species of trees and in the spring classes competed to see the most bird species. The kids had to write a detailed report on the geology and natural and human history of their property, which included interviewing an old-timer. Most of them loved it. I am still in touch with a dozen or so of my former students, now scattered around the world, on Facebook.

Commuting back and forth from the sanctuary to Harper & Row's offices on Fifty-Third Street became too much for Leslie, so she got an apartment in the city, where I refused to live. She was a city person, and I was a country boy, so we only lasted through 1974. I quit Rip after the second year and finished my book, pouring all the love I had put into the Florida book, plus the love I had no one to give to now, and in the fall of 1975, with a contract from Sierra Club Books, I set out on a nine-month tour of the Amazon, which resulted in my third book, *The Rivers Amazon.*

At the very start of the expedition, in the Brazilian state of Pará, I visited the King Ranch, whose rain forest was being converted to pasture for cattle. The trees were being cut down with chain saws, dragged down by chains between tractors, and torched—a foretaste of what Davie and I will find happening in Borneo forty years later. I stood on a hill surrounded by miles and miles of thick black smoke pouring into the sky as far as I could see. And there were fires like this all over the Amazon, one on the Volkswagen Ranch that was reported to be bigger than Belgium (an exaggeration, but the fact that such a comparison could even have been made gives an idea of how big it was).

One of my main mentors for this book and many subsequent projects was Thomas Lovejoy, a visionary tropical and conservation biologist who coined the term *biodiversity* and pioneered the debt-for-nature swap, whereby developing countries were forgiven their debts to the International Monetary Fund in return for setting aside key portions of their still-intact wilderness areas. He also devised the minimum critical ecosystem study in the rain forest outside of Manaus, to determine how much reduction a forest can take before its biodiversity begins to be compromised, and the intricate web of interactions between its plants and animals breaks down, to help the Brazilian government regulate the massive deforestation that loggers and ranchers were doing in the Amazon. Lovejoy had predicted that if the incineration of the Amazon continued the way it was going, a million species would become extinct before they were even identified. That was one of the things that got me down there: I'd better see the Amazon before it's gone.

I didn't know it until 2013, when I met some of their cousins, but there were still uncontacted bands of nomadic hunter-gatherers in the vicinity of this massive conflagration. Obviously so much thick, black smoke must be having more than a local effect, I thought, and when I got back Lovejoy put me in touch with George Woodwell at the Woods Hole Oceanographic Institution. Woodwell was a pioneer in the measurement of atmospheric CO_2 and explained to me the green-house effect, which was little known outside the climate-science community and still controversial.

In places the flames of the burning trees on the King Ranch were so hot and high that some of the trees had been sandblasted and landed upside down with their buttresses in the air like the fins of crashed rocket ships. This was the third seminal encounter in my education as an environmentalist. I didn't plan on being one. The word wasn't even in vogue yet. I was a naturalist and nature writer. I just wanted to experience the natural world and visit far-off places, but half the time, in the decades to follow, when I got to these remote Edens, they were being destroyed by the modern world's appetite for wood, oil, gold, rare minerals, and by local population growth, with its need for more farmland, charcoal, and money. Few people from my world were going to get to these places, so I felt an obligation to tell them what was happening. Increasingly, this became the mission of my writing: to evoke the beauty and fascination and preciousness of what is being laid waste to in a way that the reader starts to care and maybe even wants to do something about it.

On that first trip I went completely off the grid, back to the late Stone Age, and met hunter-gatherers living the way humans have lived for all but the last ten thousand years. But even they were planting a few crops like bananas, manioc, and papayas. Again—the story of my life, and everybody's—I caught the tail end of something. I spent a month with the Mekranoti, who wore nothing but penis sheaths and wooden lip discs—their nearest neighbors were the still-uncontacted Kreen Ak-rore, three hundred miles to the west—and made the first collection of their medicinal plants, all of which were in chemically active families, including a contraceptive the women said they took to space out their kids; one dose was good for two years. The only nonactive plant was a penis-shaped saprophyte on the forest floor, which the Mekranoti believed women had to eat to get pregnant; sex was purely recreational.

New Year's Day, 1976, I spent in a communal *maloca*, or thatch longhouse of Yanomami, near the Venezuela border that had never been entered by anybody from the outside world. Their shaman snorted the powdered hallucinogenic snuff of the *Virola* tree and as its effects came on, he became his *rishi*, his animal alter ego who was living a parallel existence to his somewhere in the forest, which can be a jaguar, a monkey, even a butterfly. In his case it was a hawk, and he flapped around the communal thatched-palm *maloca* and made piercing calls like a hawk. The Yanomami, I learned, were juggling thirteen different layers of reality, not just the physical material world that the Western rational-scientific mindset maintains is all there is (except for religious Westerners who believe in heaven and hell). This was my first of many encounters with what the Brazilian anthropologist Eduardo Viveiros de Castro calls "indigenous multiperspectivism": Europeans think there is only one reality but many ways of seeing it, while indigenous people think there are many realities but only one way of seeing them.

I had given a family of *caboclos*, mestizo river people, who were laid out with falciparum malaria my round of pills for this often fatal mosquito-borne disease, which turns your urine the color of Coca-Cola (hence its colloquial name, blackwater fever). A few weeks later, high in the Peruvian Andes, on my way up Mount Mismi, an extinct snow-covered volcano then thought to be the ultimate source of the Amazon, I contracted it myself and came within an inch of dying. I probably only survived because I was young and strong and in great shape, having just paddled up a river for eleven days then loped through the forest with Yanomami for a week. But I have permanent scars on my heart from the stress it endured, as each day the attack came punctually at noon and my temperature spiked to 104 degrees and remained there for four hours, my heart pounding all the while like a sprinter's. The local people, the Quechua, were wary and withdrawn but invariably hospitable and did what they could to help this gringo who had landed in their midst and was obviously very sick.

After several mornings of being taken from village to village, when I was still able to walk, I had a classic near-death experience. Barely making it to somebody's stone croft and collapsing on the dirt floor, I saw the radiant light at the end of the tunnel, which in my delirium was at the bottom of the Apurimac gorge, which I had just climbed down into and crossed on a rope bridge. I saw—or thought I saw—that death wasn't the end, and that it was nothing to be afraid of. Now I wonder if it wasn't a hallucination, like the out-of-body experiences people in the throes of desert thirst and mountain climbers in extremis have reported.

The radiant world at the end of the tunnel was beckoning, welcoming, but it was not my time. Next day I caught a bus to Cuzco, and after five days of which I remember nothing I came to in a hotel bed, still here. From then on I wake up each morning grateful to be alive and have tried to make the most of it. I would never have had five sons or gone on to write nine more books (including this one), so I have always felt there was a reason why I didn't die then, and this has given me a sense of purpose, fortified my heroic narrative.

When I got back, now married to Ana, the incandescently beautiful librarian at the National Indian Foundation in Brasília, I found that my Westchester book had been taken by the *New Yorker*. It was a joyous time after all the uncertainty and turbulence of my twenties. William Shawn, the magazine's legendary editor, told me cheerily at our first meeting, "We're interested in whatever you're interested in," and for the next ten years I made full use of this carte blanche and traveled to remote places like Madagascar and the Ituri Forest and the Nhamundá River, up which the fabled Amazon women were supposed to have lived. After a few years, the *New York Times* called me "consistently one of the farthest-flung of the *New Yorker*'s far-flung correspondents," and Timothy Ferris, *Rolling Stone*'s New York editor, called me "the only journalist in America who goes to places where you can't get a coke" and "a genuine citizen of the world, at home with people everywhere." The more remote indigenous people I visited, the more fascinated I became in their widely divergent and often elaborate cosmologies, and how most of them seemed to be saying that this is not the real world, but only one of many.

Visiting Madagascar in 1986, I experienced "a world apart," as the lemur primatologist Alison Jolly called this amazing archipelago below the southeastern tip of Africa. Fifty percent of its inhabitants were animists who believed that they would become crocodiles, boas, or lemurs when they died. There were ancient trees dripping with offerings from their human descendants. But the Malagasys were laying waste to their rain forest because their numbers were growing exponentially and they needed more and more land for their crops, and more and more trees to turn into charcoal. They were, in Jolly's words, "sacrificing their future so they can survive in the present." So "this insular sub-region . . . one of the most remarkable zoological districts on the globe," as the Victorian naturalist and biogeographer Alfred Russel Wallace called it, was also under assault. Species that had evolved there and were found nowhere else were going up in smoke, including ones that hadn't even been discovered.

In the pristine boreal forest of Manitoba I met Ojibway (Anishinaabe), who believed that everything, including trees and even rocks, has a spirit, and across the St. Lawrence River from Montreal, Mohawks who believed that everything has *orenda*, its own unique spiritual power—rabbits, flowers, even a song. And in the Arizona desert, Navajos who believed that every creature has a "way," a role to play and the right to be here, which must be respected. Humans must learn to "walk in beauty" like them, as they do just naturally and with perfect grace, no false moves, no delay between thought and action. A woman told me that when something bad happens, it's no accident. Either you brought it on yourself—you transgressed the "way" of some animal of natural force, or you were delinquent in a ceremony, or forgot to give thanks, or your wants got the better of you, or someone did it to you—black magic. "Like my husband, Kee Richard," she explained. "He started getting nosebleeds and went to the hospital in Flagstaff, and the doctor told him he had a tumor, he had cancer, and it had to be zapped with radiotherapy. But my aunt, who is a medicine woman, took one look at him and asked, 'Did you ever kill a porcupine?' and he said, 'Well, yes—when I was ten. One night a porcupine came up to our campfire, which was not normal. Porcupines don't do that unless something is wrong with him. So I beat it on the nose with a stick from the fire and killed it.' Kee Richard's aunt told him he had to offer turquoise and abalone to the porcupine, so he did, and he also had the radiotherapy, and his nose stopped bleeding. We never found out which cured him."

Dinétah, the land of the Navajo, was on a very different, much more ancient wavelength than the rest of America. It was a parallel universe. The landscape was sacred. Every outcrop and spring and old piñon tree had a story, as in the Australian outback, whose indigenous people traveled along "songlines" they had dreamed that took them to the places where they could connect with the spirits of their clan.

I was fascinated by all these belief systems and cosmologies and mythologies, which had arisen from local landscapes and made perfect sense in their context. Each one was part of a puzzle that I was putting together in my mind, that the Western rational scientific worldview was missing many pieces of, but the multiperspectivist worldviews of local indigenous people had, for so long they were almost second nature. I began to reinvent myself as an animist, to reconnect with the experiences I had had as a child in the Phillips' woods and see them in a new light.

In 1984 my grandmother Mopsy, who became a portrait painter after fleeing the Russian Revolution and had been such a huge influence on my life, had showed that it was possible to make a living making beautiful works of art and being your own boss and not working for the Man, died at the age of ninety-three. The last time I visited her, at her deathbed in Glen Cove Hospital, they had put tubes up her nose, but she managed to whisper, "We are all transitional characters." A few days later I was having Sunday lunch at a Brazilian writer's home forty miles north of the hospital, and I suddenly felt an inexplicable wave of nausea. This was at just the moment that Mopsy, I found out when I got home, died.

There are many such accounts, from cultures all over the world, as well as accounts of dogs getting excited and rushing to the door, at the moment their master, ten miles away, decides he is coming home. The explanation, I wouldn't learn for another thirty years, may be related to the discovery by quantum physicists that two molecules that were once connected can communicate instantly even if they are light-years away from each other.

Of course I found these "whiffs of the uncanny," as Nicholas Shakespeare calls them in his biography of Bruce Chatwin—things that Western science is not yet able to explain, but nevertheless happened and are out there—particularly interesting, especially the ones I experienced personally.

The Tarahumara people of Mexico's Sierra Madre Occidental, whom I have been to see three times, traditionally believe that males have two souls, and females four, so gays have six and are revered as shamans with special powers. They also believe that when you die, you have to retrace the footsteps of everywhere you have been and present them, along with your hair, to God. I am presenting these selected footsteps from my world travels between 1960 and 2013 to readers who might be interested in following them, although this is of course impossible, each of us having his or her own life journey to take and own heroic narrative to find and realize, and the world I have known is much changed. Many times I have returned to a pristine Eden in some far-flung corner of the globe, and found it gone, completely obliterated, or in the process of being destroyed. Humanity is overrunning the planet like a virus. But voices for the animals and plants and the indigenous subsistence cultures that evolved with them and are part of the same ecosystem are needed even more desperately.

In 1986 I wrote my first piece for the newly resurrected *Vanity Fair* (its previous incarnation having gone under in 1936) about the murder of Dian Fossey. Ana had born me two boys, Andre and Nick, only seven and six but already seasoned explorers, and I brought them along. We climbed up to her research station, between Mount Visoke and Mount Karisimbi, a few months after she was found with her skull split open by her own machete. The next morning we went to meet one of the habituated mountain gorilla families, who were in the bamboo forest below, munching stinging nettles and wild celery. There were twelve of them—Ndume, the silverback, his three mates, and their eight kids. We just hung out together, my family and Ndume's. It wasn't often that they got to meet human kids, so his kids were really curious. Ndume, who weighed about three hundred pounds and ate about forty pounds of vegetation a day, had lost his right hand in a poacher's snare. He knuckle-walked to within two feet of me and sat down, facing the other way, completely ignoring us. His head, with its massive brow ridge and powerful jaws, was huge. After fifteen minutes, he ambled over to a comfortable-looking spot and, snorting contentedly, proceeded to sack out. There he remained, dead to the world, limbs every which way, until we left. The other gorillas circled us curiously. Safari walked out to the edge of a branch and jumped up and down on it. The branch snapped, and she came tumbling down into a thicket and dropped from sight. Kosa, the subdominant male, reached up to a shrub and pulled it toward his mouth, releasing hundreds of fluffy seeds into the air. An unnamed young female walked toward us, briskly beating her chest for a few seconds (it was more like fluttering than pounding and seemed to be meant more in friendship than intimidation), sat down beside Nick, my six-year-old, put his poncho in her mouth, bashed him on the knee a couple of times, and then went over to her mother. I tried to catch a glint of recognition in the gorillas' soft brown eyes, but they remained glossed over, wild. It was clear, though, that they trusted us, maybe more than they should have, and it felt as if we all could have started a conversation, if we had only been able to find the language.

This was a major breakthrough for me. It was like Adam's Wall, as the barrier between us and other animals has been called, didn't exist. Of course I had never felt there was any barrier between me and our various dogs and cats, and these were our close primate cousins, who share from 95 to 98 percent of our genes, depending on what is counted. Only chimpanzees and bonobos are more closely related to us. The only comparable experience I had had with a primate up till then was with a spider monkey in a mangy zoo in Iquitos, Peru, ten years earlier. He looked at me imploringly from behind the bars of his cage. His message was clear: please, mister, get me out of here.

PART THREE

LEARNING FROM THE ANIMALS

Noah's Ark at the Pan

In 2011 I did a piece for *Vanity Fair* about elephants and the ivory trade called "Agony and Ivory" that took me to nine countries on three continents. In Zimbabwe I drove around Hwange National Park with Johnny Rodrigues, the fearless founder of the Zimbabwe Conservation Task Force. He took me around its "pans," the artificial, dug waterholes where the animals come to drink. "We have much to learn from the animals," he told me as we pulled up to one. "When they come to the waterholes, each species has its turn. I made a twenty-four-hour video of this pan five years ago. It showed how every animal's right to the precious fluid was respected. The predators didn't go after their prey. Elephant, giraffe, zebras, sable antelope, kudu, warthog, baboons, buffalo, lions, even hyenas and jackals—all your different species came, and each took its turn to take a drink. It was like Noah's Ark. And after all had a drink they came back a second time, each in its turn. And you say to yourself, why can't humans learn from that? We'd kill each other to get to the water."

(Or be selling tickets. Or poisoning the water in the pans with cyanide, which there has been a rash of in Hwange starting in 2013. In October 2015, forty elephants there were killed by cyanide in two separate incidents. Most of them had had their tusks hacked out. Ill-paid park rangers are suspected.)

Graydon Carter, *Vanity Fair*'s editor, was moved by this passage. He remembered how tourist elephants in Phuket, Thailand, sensed the 2004 tsunami coming twenty minutes before the first wave hit and charged up to high ground, then, leaving their charges and everyone who followed them, ran back down to save some children who had been swept away. So my next assignment was a spin-off from the elephant piece: What can we learn from the animals? It was a perfect opportunity to pull together my thoughts about animals and the interactions I had been having with them and to get up to speed on the latest scientific thinking and to take stock of my own evolving homegrown, reactive animism, and to get down with some new species.

Maybe the real question, I started to think, is, what haven't we learned from the animals? As Charles Darwin wrote in *The Descent of Man* (1871): "We have seen that the senses and intuitions, the various emotions and faculties, imitation, reason, etc., of which man boasts, may be found in an incipient, or even sometimes in a well-developed condition, in the lower animals." One hundred and forty years later, a last-ditch adaptation to reconnect with the animals and our own animality and redefine our relationship with them, part of a countermovement against the ravages of modern resource- and consumer-driven capitalism and toward a more "empathetic civilization" (which Jeremy Rifkin has a great five-minute YouTube spiel about), seemed to be happening. The Big Shift, as some were calling it, was moving forward on many fronts, from the Occupation of Wall Street to the increasing numbers of children who are becoming vegetarian because they "don't want to eat animals." In 2015, Pope Francis will emerge as its greatest voice, criticizing the "amoral consumerism" and the "perverse relationship between the developed and the developing world," which is laying waste to places like Borneo. "Nature is filled with words of love, but how can we listen to them amid constant noise, interminable and nerve-wracking distractions, or the cult of appearances?" he will ask in a radical encyclical that preaches "a new theology" of interconnection and love of nature and that all creatures are our brothers and sisters, but is in fact firmly rooted in the Franciscan tradition.

Plotting out my reporting safari— this is now 2012—I lined up a broad spectrum of people and animals to meet, starting in Maine and ending in Borneo, with stops on the way in New York State, the Grand Cayman Island, Iowa, Colorado, and California. While I was putting this together, the Arcus Foundation was hosting a roundtable at the Desmond Tutu Center in New York City called "Humans and Other Apes: Rethinking the Species Interface." New disciplines like "trans-species psychology" and "multispecies ethnography," I discovered, were extending the field of inquiry. Cognitive ethology—the study of animals' emotions and thought processes, which took off with Donald R. Griffin's *Question of Animal Awareness* (1976)—was exploding the myth of human exceptionalism, the core Western belief that only we are capable of morality, or ritual grief for our dead, or empathy. Everything we do, everything we are, as Darwin realized and anybody who has a dog or a cat knows, is actually on an evolutionary continuum. Dale Peterson's *The Moral Lives of Animals*, an excellent source for getting an idea of our present understanding of what is going on with our fellow creatures, and of how deeply indebted we are to them for virtually everything that we are, had just come out. Bernie Krause, the far-out bioacoustician I would be meeting in California, argues that morality, the social contract, which only humans were supposed to be capable of, is actually premammalian; it goes back to the birds. Mark Twain's contention in "The Damned Human Race," a scathing indictment of our flawed nature that was one of his last pieces of writing, that only humans are capable of gratuitous cruelty, has been disproven. Chimpanzees do horrible things to each other. And now there is a growing literature on posttraumatic stress in ivory orphans; teenaged elephants in South Africa who watched their mothers cut down and butchered for their tusks are forming anarchic gangs and attacking safari trucks with tourists.

Consciousness, or self-awareness (as opposed to just awareness of the outside world, but being aware of yourself in it), is something animals were not thought to have; yet recently, self-recognition—the ability to recognize a reflection of yourself in a mirror—has been documented in chimpanzees, orangutans, bottle-nosed dolphins, and now even magpies. So that's premammalian, too. In one experiment a white smudge was put on the forehead of an Asian elephant who noticed it in the mirror and removed it. One scientist told me this was evidence that elephants are capable of vanity, another dismissed this interpretation as anthropomorphic: the elephant just saw something that shouldn't be there and got rid of it. But again, for anyone whose dog yips excitedly in his dreams, the idea that animals are conscious of themselves, capable of conceiving of themselves in an imaginary situation, is hardly a revelation.

Up until recently, what we know about animals has mainly been acquired from painstaking hours of direct visual observation, in often trying conditions, rewarded by rare moments of elation, by field biologists like George Schaller, who made the baseline studies of the lion, the mountain gorilla, and the snow leopard. There were two cardinal rules: to remain as unobtrusive as possible, so as not to charge the scene; and to try one's best not to commit the ultimately unavoidable sin of anthropomorphism, of projecting human traits on to one's study species. But detached scientific visual observation only takes you so far, as evidence grows that the soundscape and the smellscape are more important for many species. And while Darwin's theory of natural selection as the mechanism that has driven the diversification of life and the adaptations of species to their ever-changing environments forms the basis for our understanding of biological life, there is a lot going on that it does not explain. Indigenous people who have been living in close contact with the other animals as integral parts of the same ecosystem for as long as their cultural memory, who have the sense of connectedness and kinship that we have lost, understand this in ways that modern Western science is still catching up with. I have learned a lot from such people, as well as from field biologists like Schaller and Iain Douglas-Hamilton and Richard Wrangham. There are many ways of knowing, and you do not even have to be a spiritual person to go along with Antoine de Saint Exupéry's contention that "what is essential is invisible to the eye." To feel and hear all the life in a forest. Still, animals' motivations often remain a mystery. In the end an elephant remains an elephant, a human remains a human. Even domestic cats retain an impenetrable wildness. I recently asked an elephant activist in LA, is it really true that elephants can read your heart? and she said, "It probably is, but I wouldn't count on it." Douglas-Hamilton, who has devoted his life to studying and saving Africa's elephants, told me he came suddenly upon a mother elephant and her calf in the forest of Samburu National Reserve, and the mother picked him up in the air with her trunk and was about to fling him to the ground and trample him, but at the last moment she apparently recognized he was a friend and put him down.

Trenton, Maine:
Heather Grierson's Interspecies Commune

In Bedford when Davie and I were growing up there was a local naturalist named Stanley Grierson who brought turtles and snakes and raccoons and other local critters to show to us at school. His daughter Heather now has a wildlife reserve in Trenton, Maine, which houses all kinds of animals, ranging from captive-born ligers to orphaned or injured moose, black bears, and coyotes brought to her by state game wardens. It's more like an interspecies commune or an extended family than your usual zoo, as Heather, who has been running the Kisma Preserve for twenty-seven years, describes it.

The minute I walked into Kisma Preserve, I was greeted by a raucous green and yellow macaw, perched in a dead tree a few feet above me. All the animals came up to the edge of their enclosures, eager to see who the new visitor was. I have to say that I have mixed feelings about any place where wild animals, or even captive-born individuals of once-wild species, are confined. Experiencing them is not the same as experiencing wild animals in their natural state. They are denied their natural behavior, which is to hunt for food and socialize, to establish territory and conduct their courtship displays and mate and feed their young, and move freely to wherever the food possibilities are best. They are spared the stress and uncertainty of having to get food and to watch their back lest they become food. But there isn't much to do in confinement, just eat, have sex if there is an opportunity, and observe (perhaps picking up even more than the field biologists) and identify and interact with their captors, so what you are getting is to some degree an interspecies form of Stockholm syndrome. At Camp Leakey in Borneo, which Biruté Mary Galdikas set up and where she lived for twenty years and did her research, one of the cooks was raped by a two-hundred-pound former captive adult male orangutan who apparently tragically forgot that he was not human.

Confined animals are not happy animals, any more than confined humans are. Rainer Maria Rilke feels for the panther pacing "in cramped circles, over and over," and Charles Ives for a leopard going "around his cage from one side then back to the other" in his 1906 song "The Cage." Even Bubbles, a twenty-six-year-old elephant who has been living with Heather's friend, an animal trainer in Myrtle Beach named Doc Antle, and has been loved and well taken care of since the age of two, has rubbed her tusks down to nothing three times during the winter months, when Antle is in Miami and she is kept in a heated barn. Wild elephants don't do that. Antle dismisses it as tantamount to a person chewing their fingernails, but I think it's because Bubbles is totally imprinted on him. She has never shown the slightest interest in interacting with other elephants. I spent a few days with Bubbles at the start of my nine-country reporting safari for the elephant piece, and will be seeing her again soon.

Nonetheless, much of what we know about animals, much of the scientific behavioral data, has come from observing animals in zoos and private facilities. Frans de Waal, the eminent expert on bonobos, has never seen one in the wild. They only live in the Congo basin, south of the main river. All he knows of these primates has been gleaned from observing those at Emory University. Katy Payne discovered elephant infrasound communication at the San Francisco Zoo, and the discovery that some giraffes emit low-frequency humming sounds while sleeping, perhaps as a form of communication, was made at three zoos in Europe.

And even if you are completely unobtrusive, if you hide behind a blind and watch creatures in the wild, there is still a human-animal interaction, because you are viewing them through your human lens, and the lenses of your particular culture, and whatever scientific methodology you are employing. And even if they can't see you, they are usually aware of you long before you are of them, through smell or sound. If they do see you, they can read your body language, facial expressions, eyes, the direction of your gaze—they've got your number. If they're reptiles, they suss you out with flicks of their tongue. And every living thing is resonating to every other one at the quantum level. Seeing something is a two-way street. The seer shapes the seen, and vice versa. So I am not feeling compromised about coming to this reserve. Orthodox mechanistic Darwinian behaviorism, which still dominates academic wildlife biology, is too confining a box, and if we're going to understand what is really going on with animals, their mental worlds, we're going to have to think out of the box. Rupert Sheldrake, Marc Bekoff, and Carl Safina have written eloquently about this, that the shibboleths are outmoded, and new discoveries that push the envelope of what can be scientifically confirmed is going on with our fellow creatures are being reported in journals like *Animal Sentience.*

A vivacious, tanned, blond fifty-year-old who goes around in bare feet in the summer, Heather Grierson grew up in Katonah, another of Bedford's hamlets, up Route 22. "Our house in Katonah was full of all kinds of creatures," she tells me. "Dead birds in the refrigerator, a recuperating frog or skunk in the bathtub. My room was filled with stuffed animals, vet charts. Everything I did had to do with animals. I was obsessed. One of my first words was not *Mom*, but *turtle*. I don't know whether it's genetic or not, but I think I was born into the right family.

"Zoos spend huge amounts of money recreating an ecologically correct habitat for the animal," Heather explains. "Then it is left alone, to cope with the isolation and the confinement, craving social interaction and freedom to roam that it isn't getting, which are the cruelest deprivations you can subject a social animal to, wild or human." So her approach is, as long as the animal isn't going to be in the wild—which is not an option for any of her charges, being captive-born exotics or local animals who've been injured or previously habituated to humans—"to make their lives as stimulating and enriching as possible, which means giving them lots of love and attention and concrete engagement." Like Doc Antle, Heather is a proponent of socialization of animals with people. "Once they're not in the wild, all bets are off. We do our best to make them interactive and social with whoever they're with.

"Growing up my dream was always to be a zookeeper," she goes on. "My idols were Jim Fowler [the host of Mutual of Omaha's *Animal Kingdom*] and Jacques Cousteau. Contact with animals, connection on a day-to-day basis, was always what I wanted. But it's an all-consuming lifestyle: six to seven days a week, a day off when you can take it so you don't go crazy. I was married and have had many men in my life, but none of them was able to stick it out, none had the commitment and they all tried to lure me away from it. And I get about the same respect as an abortionist. I've had animal activists picketing this place. They probably never picked up shit in their life. And these are animals who have been discarded and have nowhere else to go."

I meet two moose whose mothers were killed by cars. Heather got them when they were less than forty-eight hours old. The two black bears are full grown and enormous. One came from a little zoo in upstate New York that was going to give it to a circus. The other one was a problem bear, too imprinted on humans to be released. It was found as a baby swimming in a pool with kids, "and that can't happen," Heather explains, "so she was picked up by a state game warden and given to me. One of our wolves had been kept as a pet and was living on a sailboat; the other was in a pet store that was planning to pass it off as a dog. One of the coyotes was kidnapped by a kid who dug it out of a den and took it. After three months he realized this was not the right thing to do, but it was too late. The other was part of a newborn litter whose mother was shot by a hunter.

"There's a lot more going on with animals than most people realize," Heather tells me. "People underestimate them, I don't know why. There's so much evidence of their intelligence. The main thing is you have to know your animals. Animals have distinct personalities, for lack of another word, distinct behavior quirky to them that we do not want to give them credit for. Not every animal will like every human it meets. The female moose, for instance, is jealous of me because her mate, who died last winter, had the hots for me. You saw for yourself her behavior toward me. [We had gone up to her large enclosure and she didn't come up to us, and acted distinctly hostile toward Heather, giving her the dirty eyeball.] "That stems from the fact that I was very bonded with her now-deceased mate since he was two days old. To the day he died he was affectionate with me and would follow me wherever I went. You could tell where I was on the property by where he was looking. The female would try and put herself between us and drive me off. To this day, even after his death, she does not want me around. I would use the words *jealousy* or *possessiveness*. That might be criticized by those who say animals don't have emotions and are just globs of flesh and instinct."

The smartest or at least the most in-your-face animal in the park is indisputably Rasputin, a female raven someone brought in as a chick seven years ago—probably blown out of her nest—whom Heather raised. This is the only home Rasputin has ever known, her entire universe.

Ravens and other corvids—crows, magpies, jays—have the largest overall brain size of any bird, and a part of their forebrain called the hyperstriatum that enables them to make decisions and to manipulate other creatures, like calling wolves and coyotes to open up a carcass they have found so they can feed on it. British ravenologist Sylvia Bruce Wilmore maintains they are "quicker on the uptake" than some of the mammals we credit with high intelligence.

"Rasputin has an extensive vocabulary of human words and animal sounds," Heather tells me. "This is typical for a raven in contact with people, but I see more than just mimicry. Hard scientists and those who think animals are one-dimensional won't agree, but I have seen and heard too much to go along with their reductionism. Rasputin learned the f-word from a staff member who let it out after she booby-trapped the entrance to her enclosure with a board and he got beaned by it. Then she started to use it on the visitors and it took a lot of deprogramming and suasion to get her to stop doing it. She didn't know it was an obscenity, of course, but she probably sensed that it was a powerful emotional venting about something she was not happy about, so she tried it out on the visitors to see what kind of a rise it would get out of them. She likes to mess with you. And eventually after repeated expressions of disapproval from the staff, she got the message and deleted it from her vocabulary. But she still comes out with it on occasion. Rasputin says whatever she wants."

Rasputin particularly likes to mess with Ulrok, the Rottweiler who hangs around Heather's house and is currently being the surrogate parent for a tiger cub Heather got from Doc Antle, which seems to be going great. There are many cases of cross-species parenting, the most famous being a 130-year-old Seychelles tortoise named Mzee, who took care of a baby hippo that was washed down a river and stranded on a reef by the receding tidal wave of the 2004 tsunami. Paula Kahumbu, a protégé of Richard Leakey, the heroic Kenyan wildlife conservationist, wrote a best-selling children's book about the pair.

When Ulrok is in earshot, Heather tells me, "Rasputin will lie on her side and look like something is wrong, and pathetically say, 'Ulrok, Ulrok, help me.' When the dog goes to investigate, *wham*! Rasputin pecks him on the nose. Nobody taught her this and she doesn't do it with the other dogs and Ulrok falls for it every time. Rasputin also baits the mourning doves with food so they put their heads through the mesh of her cage and she grabs them by the neck and eats them. All I can say is that I firmly believe each animal is an individual and needs to be treated as such. I think it does a great disservice to overlook that and look at an animal as simply a lump of DNA, as one of a species. There is so much more."

There was a chimp in the Chicago Zoo who would pile up stones in his cage in anticipation of the arrival of the thousands of daily visitors whom he would then pelt with them. This was accepted by the hard scientists, after much debate, as evidence that chimpanzees are capable of planning ahead. Clearly Rasputin also has this ability, not to mention cunning and guile. Another nail in the coffin of human exceptionalism: We didn't come up with duplicity. But we certainly ran with it.

I go into Rasputin's enclosure and sit on a bucket a few yards from her and just let her get used to my presence, acting like I just happen to have popped in, don't mind me, it's cool, I'm up for whatever you're up for, if you're not up for anything, that's fine too. I don't make direct eye contact, so she won't feel threatened or rushed, and act like I have all the time in the world. Like the Maasai warrior who says to the tourist, "You got the watch and I got the time." I just relax into the situation, turn off the internal monologue, get rid of any preconceptions or random racing thoughts and try to settle into Rasputin's time and space, her specific sensory *umwelt*. But she is wary. Nonchalantly, to disguise what she is really thinking, like who is this guy and what is he doing in my cage, she picks up a stick with her beak and hops circuitously to within a yard closer. But she never lets down her guard. I can't even get her to say "baby bird," which Heather has no trouble coaxing out of her. I sit there for more than an hour. The sun begins to set, and a flock of noisy starlings drops into the weeping willow tree over Rasputin's nightly roost.

So my afternoon with Rasputin is a bust. She and I are doing a dance, I trying to get inside her head, she clamming up. I don't get a thing out her. After I leave her cage Heather passes it and she explodes with "baby bird," followed by a string of expletives and every other word she knows, goes completely nuts. If I may indulge in shameless anthropomorphic speculation, she was probably saying, who was that guy and what was he doing in my cage? No disputin' Rasputin is very clever and mischievous. She was acting totally in character. In many cultures Raven, like Coyote, is a trickster.

I spend the morning with two diminutive, incurably curious common marmosets, only seven inches tall and gray with white tufts and long tails. I have seen a lot of them in Brazil, mostly recently on a golf course in Rio, where they had come down from the coastal rain forest to one of the tees and seemed to just want to get to know us. They are way more advanced than the lemurs but not as smart as, say, spider monkeys. Both marmosets are very hyper and have distinct personalities. One is a more adventurous risk taker. He will take a bit of pumpernickel from my finger. The other won't. I have to put it on a branch and draw back. Both keep scampering out of the cage through a pipe to their outdoor cage and running back, dying of curiosity, especially when I start picking my guitalele, which I have brought to try to give them a little musical enrichment and to see if I can strike a common chord with them. Music is a major thing we have learned from the animals. This spring I had an exchange with a migrating thrush in our back alley. It was maybe 150 yards away up in a tree and was singing in three sets of six liquid fluted descending notes followed by a wheezy rattle of what seemed to be self-mockery. The fluted notes were in the minor pentatonic scale, which is what thrushes sing in, and is one of the common structures of all the world's music. The commentary—"wasn't that ridiculous," the wheezy rattle seemed to be saying (this is pure anthropomorphic speculation, of course)—suggested it had a degree of self-awareness, a sense of humor about itself. I answered the notes on my guitalele, and we had a little back and forth, maybe six exchanges, until it realized this is definitely not a thrush, not one of us, and clammed up.

I play the marmosets the descending call of the common potoo, a nocturnal, nightjar-like bird of the neotropics, which is in the blues scale: D–C–B-flat–G–F–D. No reaction. I try the pentatonic scale of the forest harp of the Babendjele Pygmies of Central Africa: G–A–C–D–F–G, the same box that B. B. King did most of his improvising in. Still nothing. They keep scampering out into their outdoor cage and returning agitatedly. Finally I find something completely by accident, a random fingering of two notes, B-flat to A on the first string, that immediately gets to them. They come right down to the branch a foot from my eyes and sway back and forth in unison, jostling each other. They love it, can't have enough of it. I try the same two notes an octave lower, on the third string, and it does nothing for them. So it is not just a matter of pitch, but frequency. Why do these two notes have such an effect on these two marmosets? I wonder. What does this mean? Do all marmosets have the same response? At this point this is just an anecdotal report, statistically and scientifically worthless. But the semiotics of animal musicality is not even a field that exists, and music as a way to break through with other species is little investigated—though there's a documentary on the parrots of Telegraph Hill in San Francisco, one of whom is named Mingus by the guy who made it, because when he plays his guitar and sings for him, the parrot dances in time to the music—and I'm the first to admit I don't know what I'm doing.

My next visit is with Natasha, an old lynx with rickets, literally on her last legs, not long for this world. She is in a back cage overgrown with brambles, not in public view. I enter and sit on a log and she recedes into the thicket, but not for a second does she take her eyes off me. I wear her down with my utter aloofness and gradually she creeps out to investigate. A strange man sitting in her cage is not something that happens every day; Natasha has to make sure I'm harmless. This takes about fifteen minutes. I turn my back on her and break open a book from Heather's library, George Page's *Inside the Animal Mind.* Page was the host and creator of the PBS show *Nature,* now in its thirtieth season. He died in 2006. The book was published in 1999 and is a good summary of what was known about animals' intellects and emotional lives up till then. But a lot has been learned since, and we're still just at the tip of the iceberg.

At that point, the lid had just been blown off the notion that only humans use tools with the discovery that ants use leaves as bridges over water, woodpecker finches dig for grubs with sticks, bonobos use sticks to knock down fruit or pole-vault over water, and even more impressively, Tanzanian chimps not only use twigs to fish for termites, but self-medicate with leaves of *Aspilia,* which have antibiotic properties.

Page traces how for about a hundred years the behaviorist tradition of psychology in the United States and Europe argued these animals have no "mind." Any belief to the contrary was "folk psychology"—blatant anthropomorphism. But this, Page says, is reductive. Odysseus's dog Argos recognized him instantly after an absence of twenty years when he walked into the court of Ithaca. If we could get into animals' minds, and we can't even get into each other's, we would feel right at home.

I look up. Natasha is relaxing, but still not taking her eyes off me. Page writes that we have a primordial need for our fellow creatures. Mammalian brains, whether human or shrew, have similar structures, and seek each other out. Bowlegged from the rickets—in the wild, unable to hunt for her food, she wouldn't still be alive—Natasha approaches very cautiously and nips my knee to see if I flinch, which I do, and she withdraws and plays the aloof game, yawning nonchalantly and rubbing her cheeks on a branch for a few minutes, then creeps back to bite me again and I say no and lean my bulk toward her in emphasis and she backs off.

After an hour of fending off Natasha, who keeps wanting to nip me, I go in with Saskya, a younger adult lynx who was all over me yesterday, presenting her arched back to be scratched and butting me with her head but is now fixated on the serval that has just been put in an enclosure across the yard. I sit on a bucket, and after she has studied the serval to her satisfaction, she comes over to me in her own sweet time and head butts me affectionately and presents her back for scratching, then she goes up on a platform and returns to the slab of meat and bone she had been crunching up. But at all times she is acutely alert; her tall erected black-fringed, white-tipped ears are constantly moving around like scanning radar. A pin drops on the premises, a sparrow calls in the distant woods, and she picks it up. And Saskya is captive-born, so this hypersensitivity to everything that is going on is instinctual, congenital.

Heather tells me, "Animals don't make false moves. There's no wasted motion. They ground you and remind you of what is real. A snake slithering through the grass is poetry in motion, like the most beautiful ballet. Animals give you a communication deeper than words, which you can hide behind and play games with. They are no less intelligent, but they think with their senses, and we think in language. Animals that have time to sit around and watch things don't have all these other things going on. Most people are not really focused on the task at hand. A really good fisherman—I've been out with a few on their boats—is focused on real things. But that kind of focus is rare—in the modern world at least."

A Hug from Bubbles at Bhagavan Antle's TIGERS, South Carolina

A few days later, I am down in South Carolina and stop to say hello to Bubbles, the resident elephant at TIGERS, the Institute for Greatly Endangered and Rare Species, located in Myrtle Beach and founded by Doc Antle. Bubbles and I spent two days together the previous fall, swimming in the intercoastal waterway, poking around in the woods. I had wanted to get down with an elephant before embarking on my reporting safari, and Heather had said I should go down and see Bubbles again.

Bubbles was orphaned during the last elephanticide, in the 1980s, when booming Japan's yen for ivory was the problem. When she was two, her mother was shot in Zimbabwe, and she was adopted by Antle, who trained her to be in movies and TV commercials. Supersmart, often anticipating the director's commands, she was in *Doctor Dolittle* with Eddie Murphy and the second Ace Ventura movie and a Janet Jackson video. Now, having just turned twenty-nine and retired from the silver screen, she is one of the stars of TIGERS' daily exotic animal show, "the only contact elephant in the West," Antle's son-in-law, Adarsh tells me, the only elephant the public is allowed to touch. Both Antle and Adarsh are American Hindus who changed their names, followers of the late Swami Satchidananda, the bushy-bearded guru who gave the opening blessing at Woodstock. The Hindu reverence for animals and belief in the kinship of all living things, the notion that we are all fungible, temporary consciousness housings, no matter what species we are and what body we happen to be inhabiting, is one of the underlying concepts of this unusual and controversial operation, which, it has to be said, is not held in high regard by the animal-rights community. One activist told me it is "the worst," and chastised me for having anything to do with it. But Bubbles is totally habituated to humans so I figured she was the perfect elephant to start with, and she was. Plus I didn't know before I went that TIGERS was held in such bad odor by the activists, and now that I've been there twice, I don't agree with them.

Seventy to eighty people a day pay $250 apiece to meet Bubbles and the other animals who live in the fifty-five-acre "preservation center." Antle reckons she has interacted with seven thousand or eight thousand people since I hung out with her nine months ago. I wonder if she is going to remember me.

Antle wants me to take in this year's show, which is all about conservation. "I'm a wildlife conservation guy who tries to do it in a different way, to let people have the personal experience and connection with wild animals," he explains. "The greatest video on National Geographic only goes so far. When you touch Bubbles and feel her hairy, leathery cracked skin, that ivory in your hand, and see that she is a bright, shining intellect and feel her sniffing you out, reading your heart, with her trunk, it makes the wildlife and nature we are destroying real." Antle donates 30 percent of TIGERS' proceeds to hands-on conservation projects in Thailand, Borneo, Africa, and South America that are helping to sustain the remaining tigers, orangutans, elephants, cheetahs, and jaguars in the wild.

Adarsh is presenting "the greatest hands-on animal show on Earth," as he calls it. As we watch from the safety of a balcony a young tiger cutting loose at fifty miles an hour after a "mopalope," a mop pulled speedily by a wire, he says, "now there are fifteen hundred tigers in India, surrounded by over a billion people." Later, after we are all seated and a binturong, a strange nocturnal relative of the civet cat that lives in Asian rain forest canopies, has slunk over all our laps, some of the women and kids recoiling in fear, he quotes "the great naturalist Chief Seattle, who said one hundred and sixty years ago: 'We admire them, we fear them, they are our wild side, the hunter spirit of our dreams. We share an ancient past with these great beasts that now we seem so determined to extinguish, and just like the reflection in their amber eyes our fates are linked, and when those eyes are closed forever the world will be a much lonelier, and less wonderful place.'" Except that the chief never said this. He did give a speech in 1854, but it was embellished by a Wild West adventure writer who was playing to white Americans' conscience-stricken mythologization of the noble savage.

After the show, I tell Adarsh, "You sure laid on the conservation message loud and clear," and he says, "If you can change the way people feel, you have a chance of changing the way they think." But we all know how hard a sell it is, especially these days with so many social and environmental problems closer to home, to get people to care about what's happening to the rain forest and the wildlife in distant parts of the world most of them are never going to get to.

Toward the end of the show, Bubbles, with Antle riding her, emerges from a thicket into a little clearing a hundred feet from where the seventy of us are standing. Bubbles immediately zooms in on me, points her raised twitching trunk right at me, and her ears start to flap excitedly, and when my turn comes to go up to her and give her a carrot, she wraps her trunk around me and pulls me to her breast and raises her right foot for me to rest on. Antle tells me later that he's only seen her do this three times. One was with a little girl who had a terrible family situation and was completely lost and alone. "She was bringing you in," he explains. "You are someone she made a deep connection with and wanted to reinforce it months later. You got the extreme experience of 'we're buddies.' Animals have a way of bringing out a level of emotion and love, and until you've returned the love of an elephant—or a dog—you haven't experienced the full selfless dimension of love. They make us more human." He thinks the initial recognition was probably visual, "but not your face as much as your whole body, the way you were standing, your physical presentation, and the minute she saw you, she suctioned on to you, vacuumed you up."

I already know about this effusive hug because it was just what a wild elephant named Tusker used to give Johnny Rodrigues, the gutsy Zimbabwean conservationist who videoed the water hole in Hwange National Park. "The first elephant I got to know was Tusker," Rodrigues told me as we were driving around looking for elephants a few weeks after I met Bubbles. "We were friends for over thirty years. He used to hang around the campground in Chirare and take the campers' citrus fruits. He was always friendly and full of mischief, but wild, but I could communicate with him. I used to get calls that he was in the campground, and when he saw me he would come up to me and wrap his trunk around my neck and pull me to him and raise his right leg, which meant that he was accepting and protecting me, and I would escort him from the campground and he would follow me like a puppy. But one day in 2005," he added bitterly, "the manager of the campground got someone from National Parks to shoot him."

Elephants' empathy, as well as their phenomenal memory, is thought to be related to the abundance of "spindle cells" in their huge, convoluted temporal lobes, particularly in their hippocampus, and their trunks and the soles of their feet have an abundance of other cells known as Pacinian corpuscles that enable them to detect distant vibrations in the ground, like the rumble of thunder or an infrasound riff from another elephant miles away. The trunk, as Adarsh pointed out, has fifty thousand separate muscles, and is one of the most versatile sensory organs and appendages in the animal kingdom. But the truth is, there is a lot we don't know about the elephants. As Andrea Turkalo, who has since 1990 been observing four thousand forest elephants in the *bai*, a protected clearing in the Central African Republic that was the last stop in last year's elephant reporting safari, told me, "As far as really understanding them goes, I feel like the Wright brothers when they were still trying to design a plane that would stay in the air." But there is a growing body of evidence suggesting that elephants have better memories than we do, and that they are more empathetic and by some measures even more intelligent. The Dalai Lama didn't remember me when I went to see him again several years after a two-hour private audience with him in 1990 that was seminal to my understanding of the core Buddhist belief in *shunyata*, the lack of independent existence or reality of anything, but Bubbles did, right away, and I was with seventy other people.

And the tragedy is that just as we are finally beginning to make significant breakthroughs, the elephants and all the big, free-roaming species are being slaughtered. Only around twenty-five thousand lions are left in the wild, and the same number of rhinoceroses. I saw several of the last thirty northern white rhinos in the wild in Garamba National Park, in the Democratic Republic of the Congo, bordering Sudan, in 2001. They were subsequently wiped out by the Lord's Resistance Army and the subspecies is extinct in the wild. There are currently only seven northern white rhinos left on Earth: four that were moved from a zoo in the Czech Republic to Kenya's Ol Pejeta Conservancy in 2009, and three that are still there. So when Antle calls his facility a *preservation center*, even though almost all of the animals in his menagerie are captive-born and would not last much longer in the wild than we would, the term is appropriate. It was here that he rebred the "tabby" strain of Bengal tiger, thought to have been extinct, from a tiger found with two hundred other animals in an abandoned zoo in Uttar Pradesh that Mother Teresa told him about in the early 1970s.

How could we be so ruthlessly and relentlessly destroying our own home, and systematically annihilating its other denizens, our fellow creatures who have so much to contribute to the richness of our existence and in many cases have been here much longer than us? In his 1982 book, *Nature and Madness*, Paul Shepard suggested that modern humanity is in the grip of a societal psychosis, which we are taking out on the natural world, which we were grounded in for most of our history but have been getting increasingly alienated from since the agricultural revolution ten thousand years ago. During the millions of years 38 billion of us were hunter-gatherers, we were in intimate contact with the animals. We hunted them, we followed them, we imitated their sounds and created our own music from them. They were our first teachers. We saw how they had families, how the mothers cared for their young, we watched their courtship displays and dances and imitated them. We learned their "way," as the Navajos call it, how each species makes its living in the world and contributes to its ecosystem, and how to respect its particular space and etiquette. We organized our own societies around rites of passage marking the same life stages—birth, reproduction, death—that they go through. We told our children animal fables that taught them how to behave. We identified with animals and sometimes even became them, trance-dancing ourselves into theriomorphs in the case of the Kalahari bushmen; snorting the hallucinogenic powdered resin of the Virola tree and becoming our rishi in the case of the Yanomami of the Brazilian Amazon; worshipping lemurs, boas, and butterflies as our ancestors in the case of the Malagasys.

But as we domesticated the animals and plants that provided us with a reliable source of food, we became more urban and sedentary. As grain became a hoardable source of wealth and money entered the picture, our society became stratified and hierarchical, different polities started making war on each other, and our religious life followed this pattern of centralization and institutionalization. The second Council of Nicaea (AD 787) banned the worship of nature goddesses and animal spirits, and from then on we bowed down to the Big Guy in the Sky, and only Him. The Book of Genesis sent the unfortunate message that everything on the planet, animal, vegetable, or mineral, was there for us, free for the taking, and separated us from the animals, putting them on a lower rung of the creation and giving us "dominion" over the earth. The animists believed that animals had souls, but Descartes said they didn't, which was why they were unable to feel pain. But of course, they do.

With God's blessing, the slaughter began. The Romans scalped their peninsula, hastening the demise of their empire, and in the centuries that followed the rest of Europe was denuded of trees and its game was hunted out, then the same thing happened in North America, and now the rain forests in the Amazon and Congo basins and in Southeast Asia are being chainsawed and torched.

In the last twenty to thirty years, the pace of the destruction has dramatically accelerated and the wildest, most remote fastnesses of the planet, which harbor the last large populations of wild animals, have been penetrated and are under attack. The main causes of this destruction are

1. the inexorable Malthusian math of our ever-multiplying numbers (as I write this the world's population is just hitting the seven billion mark);
2. increasing numbers of us wanting and being able to acquire the material conveniences of the modern Western lifestyle;
3. the corporate greed of multinational conglomerates whose main interest is in maximizing profit;
4. the ever-improving technology of destruction and resource extraction; and
5. inefficient and toxic methods of food production, beef being the most wasteful.

The big mammals, the apex species at the top of their food chains, are powerless against our AK-47s and other high-caliber weapons, and we want their habitat, or their gallbladders, or their ivory, so they are the first to be sacrificed. But the songbirds, frogs, bats, bees, and freshwater clams are also experiencing massive die-offs for reasons that are not clear but directly or indirectly have to do with our impacts on their environments (habitat loss, industrial chemicals). Then there is the game changer of global warming: over the next hundred years, many scientists predict, if the temperature rises 3.6 to 5.4 degrees Fahrenheit, 20 to 30 percent of species could be lost. If the most extreme warming predictions are realized, the loss could be over 50 percent, according to the United Nations' Intergovernmental Panel on Climate Change. And half the individual animals alive in 1970 have already been killed.

As Pat Awori, a Kenyan wildlife activist, told me, "We are the first generation to have lost the connection with the animals. Now we are in competition with them." Kenya's population, now around forty million, more than doubled in the last thirty years, while the elephant population was cut by more than half. The Kikuyu and Maasai still had reverence for the animals, especially for the elephants, which they believed had souls like us. That has all but disappeared when pitted against poverty and the quick bucks that can be made from poaching.

Heather Pepe, a sea turtle conservationist who has seen a similar deterioration of the local culture on the island of Tobago, wrote to me of the changes she's seen. In the early nineties, when Heather moved there, Tobago was a laid-back, sunny island based on barter and subsistence fishing and farming. The Tobagans caught green turtles, but if a female came up on a beach to lay her eggs, her right to reproduce was respected, and she was left alone. But then the cash economy and the modern consumer culture arrived. Everything became about money. The young men lost their respect for the turtles and now they kill them on sight, even gravid females, and sometimes even torture and mutilate them "out of spite," Heather writes, because the green turtles have been declared endangered and they aren't allowed to take them anymore, and their once sane, sustainable way of life is gone and they have become ghettoized in their own island paradise, and guns and drugs have arrived, compounding the poverty, so the young men are taking out their anger and frustration at the hopelessness of their lives on the turtles. The turtles are victims of Shepard's "societal psychosis."

So this is why we are destroying our earthly home and our fellow creatures—out of spite? Because our conquest of nature has backfired horribly, unleashing floods and droughts and hurricanes, and we've become a sick, vindictive society, "strik[ing] back at a natural world that we dimly perceive as having failed us," Shepard writes. We can't stop the processes that we've unleashed, so we're taking what we can while the getting is good without the slightest moral compunction, which is possible because we're so desensitized, spending our waking hours in front of screens, suffering from what Richard Louv has called "nature-deficit disorder." Suits in New York, London, and Singapore are signing the death warrants of forests and wildlife on the other side of the planet that they have never seen and never will. But what the Australian environmental scientist Glenn Albrecht has termed *solastalgia*, "the pain experienced when there is recognition that the place where one resides and that one loves is under immediate assault," is eating at our "ecological unconsciousness." And we still have our innate biophilia, however undernourished it is of late. We've definitely lost our moral compass. Maybe the animals can get us back on track.

Animals Who Heal: Prancing Horse, North Carolina, and Dolphin Human Therapy, Grand Cayman Island

In fact, animals are being used for therapy. A certified speech therapy dog in Atlanta named Ernie has helped three hundred to four hundred children overcome their difficulties pronouncing words, simply by listening to them read aloud to him, because Ernie is someone they are totally comfortable with, someone they know will not judge them if they say a word wrong. Dogs are being used in maximum-security prisons in at least twenty states to socialize violent criminals, to give them often the first unconditional love and devotion they have ever known. Some of the dogs are "unadoptable," with behavioral issues of their own, so they and the prisoners are healing each other.

Horses, whose relationship with humans is as close and ancient as dogs', are also being used for therapy. Worldwide there are more than eight hundred PATH (Professional Association of Therapeutic Horsemanship) horse therapy centers. Within three hours of each other in North Carolina are a horse therapy center for Iraq vets with PTSD (posttraumatic stress disorder), one for teens at risk for violent behavior, and one called Prancing Horse for children with physical or cognitive problems, which I visited on the way down to see Bubbles. There I spoke with horse therapist Malaika King Albrecht, whose daughter Serena has aphasia. As a child she couldn't speak, now at nine she barely can. But the moment Serena got on Cee Bar, a twenty-two-year-old mare, she underwent a remarkable transformation and became extremely verbal and articulate. Yet the minute she got off Cee Bar, she went back into aphasic mode. Malaika explained that her daughter is a kinetic learner, as opposed to a visual or an auditory one. Malaika is thinking of teaching her the multiplication tables while on Cee Bar.

Another of Prancing Horse's students, Jonathan McCrann, was hemiplegic—completely paralyzed from infancy—arm, leg, trunk—on his left side. His parents brought him for therapy, and by the time he was four he was able to walk with a walker, and at six started walking on his own. "When you're on a horse that's walking, its shoulder sockets move the same as your hip joints," Malaika explained, "so you're using the same muscles to keep in balance with its gait, and walking vicariously." It's like the great warrior riders—the Mongols, the Plains Indians—who became one single animal with their horse and galloped through space together.

Equally dramatic results are being produced by the therapeutic use of Atlantic bottle-nosed dolphins for children with Down's syndrome, autism, and other neurological impairments. One of the operations is on Grand Cayman Island, which there is a direct flight to from Charlotte. My next destination on my way to Borneo.

I drive up the northwestern arm of Grand Cayman to West Bay, where Dolphin Human Therapy Grand Cayman is headquartered. Diane "Dee Dee" Sandelin, its program director, takes me down to the cove where eleven dolphins are kept. The cove is maybe one hundred by seventy-five yards and is sealed off from the sea by a breakwater except for a small, barred inlet-outlet. Dee Dee is a down-to-earth, hands-on, no-nonsense sixty-three-year-old-woman who has the glow of someone who is in close daily contact with animals and is passionate about what she does. But Diane is not an animal caregiver. It's all about the kids for her. The dolphins are only a means to an end.

On the dock I meet Gavin Percy, Leigh Cowlishaw, and their six-year-old son, Keir. They have come from Yorkshire for two weeks of dolphin therapy for Keir, a precocious, intelligent-looking kid. "Keir has cerebral palsy and autistic tendencies that affect his behavior and right-side mobility," Leigh explains. "His behavior is aggressive to his brother and me. He punches, kicks, bites, and spits on us. He wants his own way. I think we've been too soft on him. He's controlling our lives. We want to learn techniques to help him get over it. We've been on a big roller coaster since his birth."

This morning, Keir is working with a dolphin named Nemo. Halfway through the session, they are seeing remarkable changes in Keir's behavior. "Being able to swim and play with the dolphins is an amazing incentive," Leigh tells me. "He's learning, without knowing it, a different way to deal with anger."

"The warm water and sun alone are therapeutic," Gavin adds.

At a clap from Jeremy, the young Jamaican trainer, Nemo swims up to the dock and turns on his side and waves "hi" with one of his flippers. Keir touches Nemo's nostrum. He's learning all the parts. Belly, tail, fluke, the cantaloupe-size nostrum, also known as the melon. Nemo lies on his back and Keir grabs his pectoral fins and off they go for a spin around the cove. Keir is in seventh heaven. What a way to connect with the world, and without his being aware of it, with his impaired right side.

This place illustrates spectacularly what contact with our fellow creatures can do for you, and how starved modern kids, many of whom are suffering from nature deficit, are for it.

Panbanisha, in the Great Ape Trust with Sue Savage-Rumbaugh

A few days later, I am sitting on a little island on a little lake outside of Des Moines, Iowa, with a twenty-five-year-old bonobo named Panbanisha and a sixty-five-year-old woman named Sue Savage-Rumbaugh. They have spent almost every day together since Panbanisha was born, in captivity in Atlanta, and are each other's closest friends in the world. The two of them are looking out together across the lake to the endless flat pastoral beauty of the heartland. It is late in the afternoon, and the sun is beginning to sink into the clouds on the faraway horizon. Their profiles are remarkably similar, like an old couple who have come to resemble each other, but also because bonobos and chimpanzees are our closest hominid relatives. We share 96 to 98.8 percent of our genes with them, depending on what is counted, and bonobos are more gracile, slender, and proportioned like us, compared to the more robust chimps, and their faces are longer and more human looking than the chimps with their prominent brow ridges. If there is an Adam's Wall between Panbanisha and Sue, it is cellophane thin. There is no language barrier because they communicate through four hundred lexigrams they developed together. They probably communicate better than most human couples.

Panbanisha starts to make a series of long, mournful hoots. Sue explains that a train is coming. She hears its whistle before we do. After several minutes an interminable freight train passes on the other side of the lake, and after several more minutes the long-gone engine lets out the same series of long, mournful hoots. The sound of freedom, of the road, of the big world out there beckoning for many a young person longing to extricate himself from the hinterland. I wonder what Panbanisha makes of it.

It starts to rain. Sue points to a picture on Panbanisha's panel and says what it means: Do you want to go inside now? And Panbanisha silently points to the picture that means yes.

Susan Savage-Rumbaugh is the chief scientist at the Great Ape Trust, started in 2007 by Ted Townsend, whose father, Ray, had made millions from his inventions, the Frank-O-Matic, which automatically mass produces hot dogs, and another machine that strips the skin off hogs. Ted got interested in bonobos and sold the family company that year. Georgia State University was getting out of the ape research business, and he acquired its seven bonobos and two orangutans and hired Dr. Rumbaugh, the head of its Language Research Center. The trust is a private, independent entity funded by Ted, who is now in his eighties. It takes up 230 acres on the southeastern limits of Des Moines, including a 30-acre lake in the middle of which is a heavily secured concrete pillbox that you can drive to on a spit. This is where the apes live. It feels like going to see Hannibal Lecter, or the inmates of some very special maximum-security prison. The BBC was just here, Sue tells me. They're doing two one-hour shows on animal Einsteins.

Sue is three months older than me. She grew up in Springfield, Missouri, and in the early sixties became interested in psychology and the behaviorism of B. F. Skinner, and was on her way to Harvard to become his graduate student when she visited a friend at the University of Oklahoma, where the first work was being done on teaching apes sign language. Skinner's central thesis, that the definant of man is language, she realized, was wrong. Eventually she taught her bonobos 400 lexigrams. This is how they communicate. "They understand our language much better than we do theirs," she says. "That's the next step." Koko, a western lowland gorilla in San Diego who has been taught more than a thousand signs by her trainer, Francine "Penny" Patterson, in what Patterson calls "Gorilla Sign Language" (GSL), and can understand approximately two thousand words of spoken English, had a cat she was very tight with. The cat died, and Koko, who had never experienced death, signed to Patterson the words meaning "deep dark hole."

Sue says the people in Wamba, Congo, where the Japanese have a bonobo research station, say bonobos have souls and practice animism and that when God passed out all the faces, the bonobos got there late, which is why they are not as pretty as other humans, but they definitely think of them as a form of people, that we were formerly brothers.

The ancestors of the genus *Pan*, to which chimpanzees (*P. troglodytes*) and bonobos (*P. paniscus*) belong, split with those of humans four to six million years ago, and two million years ago, the creation of the Congo River separated the ones who became bonobos on the south side of the river. While chimpanzees are discontinuously distributed across Equatorial Africa and number about 150,000 to 200,000, there are only maybe 20,000 to 40,000 bonobos left in the wild. They've been decimated by hungry humans in the ongoing sixteen-year civil war in the Democratic Republic of the Congo, and most recently by ivory poachers. They are much more peaceful than chimpanzees, maybe because by the time they were segregated by the river, gorillas had died out on their side and there was no niche competition, so bonobos became gentler and more vegetarian. They aren't into gang warfare like male chimps. Bonobo males are less physically aggressive and powerful than chimp males. Their society is matriarchal: the females control the male with access and denial of sex. If a male gets out of control, the females gang up and put him in his place. But more often, intergroup or individual tensions are mediated and defused by simply having sex. Bonobos have a "*Kama Sutra* of erotic possibility," as Dale Peterson writes, including French kissing, oral sex, anal sex, same-sex sex, female-to-female clitoris rubbing, penis to penis, even the missionary position—one more thing we didn't come up with, one more nail in the coffin of human exceptionalism. Bonobos have been called the "make peace not war" and "the hippie ape." Sue tells me there are three novels about the future race of Earth being bonobo-human hybrids, the idea being that having a shot of bonobo would make us nicer. Unfortunately we seem to take after chimps. Warfare—violent conflict over resources like fruits trees—predates Homo sapiens. Another thing we didn't invent.

A few years ago, she says, one lab actually succeeded in producing a bonobo-human clone, but the scientists aborted it for fear of what they could be unleashing on the world.

We talk about how humans are naturally attracted to animals, particularly when they are kids. There's a good book about this: *Made for Each Other: The Biology of the Human-Animal Bond*, by Meg Daley Olmert. The neurophysiological mechanisms involved are in all animals: spindle cells (as discussed previously in elephants), as well as mirror neurons, special cells first discovered in macaques that enable you to empathize and get in the heads of other beings, whether of your own species, or others. Contagious empathy is one example of behavior linked to these neurons—one kid in the classroom yawns and they all start to yawn. It has been proposed that hunters use their mirror neurons to understand the behavior of their prey and to understand how other top carnivores like leopards take down the herbivores they eat.

"And these transmissions and responses are not just happening among animals," I say, "but among plants: the envelope of what it means to be a sentient being is being pushed. Trees have been found to send each other chemical signals when there is a threat to their existence, like acacias whose canopies are being overgrazed by giraffes: they start to emit an odor giraffes can't stand, and the wind wafts it to the other acacias, and they emit it too. The giraffes outfox them by going to acacias upwind of the smelly ones that haven't gotten the message."

We fall silent, pondering these amazing discoveries and how many still have to be made before we begin to understand even how the brain produces thoughts like the ones we've been sharing, and how much of our conversation Panbanisha is picking up. "In the course of the day Panbansha's attitude toward you has shifted from 'this is someone I have to interact with,' to 'this is someone I want to get to know,'" Sue tells me.

Besides having amazing human language-acquisition skills, Panbanisha is very musical. She jammed once with Peter Gabriel. I've seen the video. Panbanisha is given a keyboard for the first time, and immediately, without any coaching, her elegant fingers find an octave, then its fifth. Gabriel plays on his keyboard some rock progressions that are not in the idiom of animal sound, but Panbanisha manages to play along. They sound like a sloppy band on psychedelics. Sue doesn't know if bonobos organize sound in the twelve-note octave and the cycles of fifths (which gives rise to the pentatonic) the way humans do. Panbanisha's musicality has not been explored, and Sue extends an invitation to return and see what common chords we could find. She asks if I would play her a tune on my guitalele—I was telling her about the marmosets for whom B-flat and A were magic notes. So I play a rousing version of "Wade in the Water," doing the refrain, "God's gonna trouble the water," over and over, which the Babendjele Pygmies I jammed with last year had really gotten off on. Panbanisha and her twelve-year-old son, Inyota, who had become agitated by my strange presence in the morning, sit raptly—Sue later tells me they were humming softly along—and when I finish the song, Sue claps, and Panbanisha and her son send up screeches of appreciation. When I tell Panbanisha "I have to go now, I hope we meet again," she rushes up to the glass that separates us and raps out with lightning-fast fingers the most extraordinary syncopated high five on it. Its meaning is clear: boogie on. We are buddies. We have connected.

From Behaviorism to Compassion, a Visit with Marc Bekoff in Boulder, Colorado

I spend the afternoon with Marc Bekoff, one of the gurus of the new cognitive ethology. Marc lives on the edge of a canyon above Boulder, Colorado, and is taking care of his neighbor's dog who hangs out, often with friends, in a dog run when he's not home, because there are mountain lions and black bears in the vicinity. He has just come back from the conference on "rethinking the species interface" in New York City, and before that he attended a conference in Wales on the importance of play in behavioral development. Marc is also sixty-five. He is originally from Brooklyn and still has a Woody Allen accent and New York intensity despite having left the metropolis decades ago to teach animal behavior at the University of Colorado.

"We had no pets when I was growing up," he tells me, "except a goldfish in a bowl because my mother had been bitten by a dog, but my folks said from the time I was three I was always asking how animals were thinking and feeling, and it was a very compassionate household. I was a conscientious objector during the Vietnam War, then I spent two years working toward my PhD at Cornell Medical School, but part of my research required killing cats, and what I really wanted to do was to study animals, not cut them up, so in 1970 I switched to Washington University in St. Louis to study wolves, coyotes, and dogs. We did captive work on the development of canid social behavior that was impossible to do in the field. Then from 1977 to 1984 I led a field project on the social behavior and ecology of the coyotes in Grand Teton National Park. They live very varied lives—alone, as mated pairs, or in packs—based on food availability. This was one of first studies of social ecology, and it showed significant within-species variability. We marked animals so we were able to show that packs were actually extended families. There was a fairly extensive network of aunts and uncles and a lot of alloparenting (helping behavior) by others in the pack. We did around five thousand hours of direct observation over eight years. We sat up on Blacktail Butte watching the coyotes from a distance and they habituated to us really fast. Donald Griffin had put cognitive ethology on the map with his 1976 book, *Question of Animal Awareness*, and I was asking questions early in my research about the importance of playing, putting forth that it could have a fitness component, but also that animals enjoyed doing it."

The study of animal behavior, Marc continues, was also heavily influenced by Skinner's behaviorism, which was a reaction against the sentimental anthropomorphism of the Victorians. Only observable behavior had cash value. The behaviorists would not say the animal is thinking or feeling, but "behaving." To Skinner and his disciples, language was "verbal behavior," love was "attachment formation," the self a "repertoire of behavior." But the new generation of field biologists like George Schaller, Iain Douglas-Hamilton, Jane Goodall, and Archie Carr Jr., who, starting in the 1950s and '60s, spent years observing animals in the wild, also saw that there were enormous differences between individuals. Not only did animals prove to have distinct personalities just like us, in the care of their young there was ample evidence of empathy and compassion, and everything they did demonstrated great intelligence, a higher sensual awareness, and the ability to be fully present. The biologists were captivated by the grace and beauty and perfection of the movements and actions of the animals they were studying, and their popular books, particularly Schaller's and Carr's, who were lyrical nature writers as well as rigorous scientists, conveyed the spiritual euphoria that being in their presence, watching them go so masterfully about their business, can induce.

Marc tells me about another new field of investigation called deep ethology. "Like deep ecology," he says, "its purpose is to help people understand we are all dependent on one another, just as all nature is. Events ripple around the world, particularly now, in the Anthropocene, when human activities are having such powerful impacts on the biosphere. Deep ethology looks deep into animals' heads and hearts, and when you do that you can't be objective. It's a movement toward uniting and breaking down species barriers. But this does not mean there aren't significant differences between us and other animals. You know the Beatles song 'I Am the Walrus'? 'I am he as you are me and we are all together.' That is what we're trying to instill. My new book, *Rewilding Our Hearts*, is all about interconnections at all different levels of human-animal interactions. In a nutshell that's what I am thinking is the future. You put it out there and do the best you can. There's a sense of urgency here," he said grimly. "We have to fucking roll. We have to be more compassionate and proactive or else this is all moot."

"Yeah," I say. "There is no Planet B."

Do you think this embracing of the animals and of our own animality could be some kind of a last-ditch adaptation? I ask him. To stop us from wiping out the last big populations of free-ranging wild animals, which we are doing everywhere, particularly in Africa?

"Animals are like us," Marc says. "They don't like to suffer, and we are harming them, so early on I became equally interested in the conservation applications of the science I was doing and helped to form the international and interdisciplinary field called 'compassionate conservation.' Science has to have an ethical component." Marc is violently opposed to laboratory experiments, circuses, and rodeos, which are "barbaric abuse of animals. Zoos I would like to see disappear and a lot of people I know who work in zoos would too."

In many books and essays Marc argues, "Let's not write volumes about the sins of anthropomorphism, but accept that this is what we do. We only anthropomorphize because we are human. Everything we see in the world is from the point of view of who we are as humans. We bring stuff to the table as individuals and evolutionarily, but it doesn't mean we shouldn't try to understand the animals, the different world of an elephant or a chimp. We have to get beyond ourselves, but there is always going to be some residue. The common denominator is that animals don't want to suffer; they want to be happy and live in peace and safety, just like we do. But if you say elephants in a zoo are unhappy, you are criticized for being anthropomorphic. But those who say the elephants are happy claim they are not being anthropomorphic. The future of the animals depends on everyone talking together. People have to realize that animals can be models of compassion and empathy. Being called an animal should be a compliment, if you realize the interconnections. There has to be a paradigm shift, a new social movement. Conservation education and humane education, like Jane Goodall's Roots & Shoots Program, have to be part of school curriculums," a point he stresses in *Rewilding Our Hearts: Building Pathways of Compassion and Coexistence*, in which he writes about "rewilding classrooms."

I think of Gandhi's observation, that one measure of the morality of a society is how it treats its animals.

"Another recent discovery is that animals can show clinical signs of depression and PTSD, just like us," he tells me. "Gay Bradshaw and others have documented teenage elephants who saw their mothers shot when they were little becoming psycho, killing rhinos and attacking tourist trucks. But there's nothing really new about this. I have seen in my fieldwork animals who could best be described as a bipolar wolf and an autistic coyote. Of course there are going to be psychopathic or sociopathic animals. If animals have joy and grief, they also can have psychological problems. But the ones that do likely don't survive. It's maladaptive. The recognition that animals can have psychosocial disorders once again lessens the gap."

Temple Grandin and Her Amazing Brain, Colorado Springs, Colorado

Temple Grandin is a really interesting person because she has the animal connection and can talk about it and its relationship to her autism, which she has done in her fascinating books *Animals in Translation*, *Animals Make Us Human*, and *Thinking in Pictures*. I drive up to Colorado Springs, where she has been professor of animal science at Colorado University's veterinary school for twenty-one years. Temple is a tall, handsome woman, a commanding presence, dressed western, like a cowgirl, and talks in a western drawl. She has grandeur and class and dignity. I'd have pegged her as the owner of some huge ranch that had been in her family for generations. She is sixty-four. You can see that she has a disability, but it doesn't diminish her. It increases her. She joins me for breakfast at the Colorado Springs Hilton, where I am staying, and tells me she grew up in an upper-middle-class family in Dedham, Massachusetts, a suburb of Boston not unlike Bedford. Her dad was in real estate and she went to Beaver Country Day School, which was not unlike Rippowam, but got kicked out for throwing a book at a girl who called her "a retard." Then she was sent to a boarding school for troubled kids in Rindge, New Hampshire. There were lot of farm animals, and the kids had to take care of them. They were "a bunch of emotionally disturbed kids living with a bunch of emotionally disturbed animals," as she writes in *Animals in Translation*. Temple had an aunt who had a ranch in Arizona, where she did a lot of riding in the summers. "Animals saved me," she tells me. "I wish more kids could ride horses today. People and animals are supposed to be together. We spent quite a long time evolving together, and we used to be partners. Now people are cut off from animals unless they have a dog or a cat.

"If you want to get kids interested in preserving these animals they have to see the real thing," she adds. "And kids want to be with animals. The Denver Zoo gets more visitors than the sports stadium."

She continues: "I am seeing flashes of New Hampshire, pictures of tobogganing, skiing, my room, the horse barn, the dairy, milking cows. They exposed me to all this farming. They didn't know it was therapeutic. Horseback riding teaches balance and rhythm. Horses are especially good for teenagers. . . . Riding a horse isn't what it looks like: it isn't a person sitting in a saddle telling the horse what to do by yanking on the reins. Real riding is a lot like ballroom dancing or maybe figure skating in pairs. It's a relationship. And taking care of a horse is a huge responsibility."

Temple has a refreshingly straightforward way of putting things, both in writing and talking. She really cuts right to the bare bones of the subject, with a kind of wisdom and real wit and down-home Will Rogers humor. The autism enables her to draw an incisive bead on what she is focusing on. "All across autism there is an area of strength and an area of deficit. I love history and know every fact about a favorite subject, for instance, and when I am tackling a scientific problem, I become completely obsessed about it, night and day, until I solve it."

As she writes in *Animals in Translation*, "Autistic people can think the way animals think. . . . Autism is a kind of way station on the road from animals to humans, which puts autistic people like me in a perfect position to translate 'animal talk' into English. I can tell people why their animals are doing the things they do." This gift gave rise to her reputation as a savant horse whisperer.

How does that work? I ask her, and she explains, "Autism is abnormalities in the white matter connecting different brain departments. At the top of the office building, the frontal cortex, are the CEO and his VPs. They use language. Deeper in the tower, on the lower floors, are visual thinking, math, music, and the emotional center, the amygdala. In autism the communication is bad." She draws the tower, slicing it into three sections: the neocortex, mammalian brain, and the reptilian brain. We have all three brains, which is why our brain has animal and human nature. As she writes, "You have your lizard brain to breath and sleep, your dog brain to form wolf packs, and your human brain to write books about it. In a lot of ways evolution is like building an addition onto your house instead of tearing down the old one and building a new one from the ground up. . . . The whole neocortex is one big association cortex."

"So because your communications with your neocortex are impaired, you are more reliant on your other brains' activity, you are more visual than verbal, which puts you closer to the animals' wavelength?" I ask, and she says, "Autistics are high fear. Psychopaths are no fear. So I don't want to do something to others that would make them afraid. So I have empathy. I don't want to make animals or people suffer. . . . I'm very high fear. I know what it is like to be in pain. Some animals are high fear, like Arabian horses, as opposed to draft horses. Labradors are a frisky, sensation-seeking breed. They will chase a ball all day long, as long as you keep throwing it. Guide dogs are more sedate and happy lying around. Some dogs tolerate being home alone, others not."

What insights have you had that are attributable to your autism? I ask, and Temple says, "If an animal has a bad experience, what it gets afraid of is very specific. People-with-black-cowboy-hats specific. I had a little dog that was afraid of hot-air balloons. There's a big event for them here every fall. Then it started getting other strange fears when I drove it around town. There'd be a gasoline tanker in front of us and it would start whining and jumping all around. Why? The gas tanker never did anything to him. Then it started getting afraid of streetlights and would throw a fit when it saw a streetlight. A stoplight was okay, cobra heads were okay, but streetlights were scary. I took five pictures—of a street light, a hot-air balloon, a gasoline tanker, and two other things it was scared of, and laid it out there on a white table in my mind. Round objects were a problem. The original trigger was hot-air balloons. Then it got afraid of other round things. So the fear was visual: a round thing against the sky. A lot of fear things tend to be visual or auditory. With cattle and horses visual is a dominant sense. They are designed to scan the horizon. Dogs are afraid of the type of shoe they were kicked with. I heard about an elephant that was terrified by a vehicle with a diesel engine; regular engines were fine. Somebody probably woke him up with construction equipment." (Or maybe poachers in a diesel truck killed his mother?)

Because she understands animal fear so well, a lot of her energies have been devoted to improving conditions in slaughterhouses. In *Thinking in Pictures* she relates how the first time she visited a kosher slaughterhouse, she heard screaming cattle from hundreds of yards away and wondered what was different in this place.

Temple became obsessed with improving the "stairway to heaven," the chute in a slaughterhouse that leads from the holding pen to the place where the cattle are killed, in the United States with a bolt gun, in the Amazon, as I have seen, with a sledgehammer blow. "A lot of people are really concerned about the systematic abuse," she says, "the slaughter of eleven billion land animals a year right here in the US, on factory farms that provide ninety-nine percent of our food. So I came up with a more merciful chute that's like a pedestrian ramp at an airport and has a squeeze box to hold them in place when they are killed. As a child on my aunt's ranch I liked to go into the 'squeeze box.' I found it calmed me, so I designed my own and used it for years as an adult."

She would agree with Bekoff that our increasing understanding of animals should translate into better treatment of them, and her humane techniques have been widely adopted.

"Give them a life worth living," she says as we drive out to her ranch. "That's the motto of the English Humane Society. See those black angus in the pasture? These beauties have a life worth living. This includes making the last few moments of life as bearable as possible. I got down and put my head where the cattles' heads were and imagined them jostling together, their agitation, sensing perhaps what was about to happen, like the line to the gas chambers. I visualized myself in the body of a cow, seeing through its eyes. These millions of animals would not exist if we were not going to eat them, so we have a responsibility to give them the best possible life. They're only here because of us and will be till the day we all become vegetarians."

Bernie Krause and the Great Animal Orchestra, Glen Ellen, California

Temple is one of the most interesting minds I have ever hung with. She has tremendous intellectual curiosity, and her own inimitable take on things, and is really interested in hearing where I was headed next: to California to visit the bioacoustician Bernie Krause who has written a groundbreaking book called *The Great Animal Orchestra* on how all our music—melody, rhythm, orchestration—comes from the animals, a thesis I have no problem with. Temple refers me to her chapter "The

Music Language" in *Animals in Translation*, which discusses the work of Dr. Con Slobodchikoff on how the language of prairie dogs is music language. "I disagree with Steven Pinker's contention that music is just so much evolutionary baggage," she says. "Why then does the brain have different areas to analyze the five different components of music, melody, rhythm, meter, tonality, and timbre? Why do so many birds and animals create music? My hypothesis is that music is the language of many animals. Music and visual come out of the more primitive parts of the brain we share with animals. Some autistic children can learn to sing before they can talk, because their singing circuits are intact."

Not only music, but dance also comes from animals. Chimps dance ecstatically at waterfalls and during thunderstorms. Aniruddh Patel at Harvard has a cockatoo named Snowball who was the first nonhuman animal conclusively demonstrated to be capable of beat induction—perceiving music and synchronizing his body movements to the beat (i.e., dancing). Each spring half a million sandhill cranes gather on the Platte River in Nebraska and do their spectacular mating dances, and in Bhutan there are ancient dances based on the dances of the cranes there. And honeybees are great dancers. When they need to find a new place for their hive, they send out scouts, and the scouts return and each party dances out the news of what they have found. As Roy Scranton writes, "Soon, in a vast rollicking chorus, masses of bees are all dancing to a variety of distinct rhythms, each dance offering a vision of tomorrow. One dance may be for a nearby oak, another for a distant elm; one dance offers an ambitious journey, another is more conservative. Over time, a single dance grows more and more popular, until a majority of bees are doing it. The swarm has made its decisions and takes flight."

Bernie Krause's home and lab are in Glen Ellen, in the heart of Sonoma County's wine country, up in the hills above the vineyards, in a magical elfin cloud forest of moss-bearded oaks and madrones and manzanitas alive with birds—everything from red-shouldered hawks to Anna's hummingbirds—whose twice-a-day concerts are backed up with a dense rhythm section of tree frogs, crickets, and cicadas. Bernie and his wife, Kat, a lovely gentle woman who is deeply involved in the battle for the Arctic National Wildlife Refuge, although she has never been there, have no kids, but a bunch of "domestic critters," as Bernie calls them: "Our cats, YoYo Meow, Eddie-Puss-Rex. Our chickens: Hen E. Youngman, Attila the Hen, Chick Corea. Then there are our new fish: Tommy Dorsal and Ella Fishgerald."

In our first conversation, by phone, Bernie laid out his basic thesis that all our music—its harmonies, orchestration, and rhythm, come from the animals. I had told him that I always took a little traveling guitar on my trips to jam with the locals and had come to recognize what I called the universal sound of music, the sound of our spiritual, romantic, and sexual longing, of our aloneness, in just about every culture's music I heard. It's in the blues, in Brazilian samba, Cuban music, in Russian music, Celtic music, Native American wailing, Chinese and Japanese music, and is basically the minor pentatonic. But I always assumed it came from some human society and spread around the world from there.

At that point, Bernie said, "Wanna hear a bird sing the blues?"

"Sure," I said.

And he played me a recording from his archive of the common potoo (*Nyctibius griseus*) made by Ted Parker III of Louisiana State University. I knew that bird from the Amazon, a brown nocturnal bird in the nightjar family that sits so still on dead stumps during the daytime that you can walk right by and not notice it. Danged if the potoo didn't cut loose with five lugubrious descending notes, D–C–B-flat–G–D—the minor pentatonic in D—that sounded just like the blues. This blew my mind, because, to continue the story of my quest to find the source of this universal sound in music, I was still thinking it must be humans somewhere who came up with it. And my quest had taken me to Bamako, Mali, touted as the birthplace of the blues, and from there to Rajasthan, India, where the diaspora of the musicians who became the Roma, or gypsies, began a thousand years ago. Then I jammed with that thrush in the back alley and found out from F. Schuyler Mathews's *Field Book of Wild Birds and Their Music* that thrushes sing in the minor pentatonic. So do all the great songsters: the musician wren, or *uirapurú*, of the Amazon, the nightingale of Europe and Russia, the bulbuls of Asia. Not only humans, but all mammals, and birds, organize sound in the twelve-note octave, which gives rise to the cycle of fifths, which gives rise to the pentatonic, which is found in the music of every culture because it's easier to remember a five-note scale than an eight-note one. But was Bernie right that we got our music from the animals, from what he called the "biophony," our melodies from the birds, our percussion from the insects, and our bass section from the frogs?

Bernie breaks the soundscape down into the biophony, the animal sounds; the geophony, earth sounds like wind, rain, running water, thunder; and the anthrophony, which is us: everything from Beethoven to the shriek of a police siren. It dominates the urban soundscape and is increasingly usurping the natural soundscape here in the Anthropocene.

On one recording safari, Bernie went to Yandoumbe in Central Africa, to the village of Babendjele Pygmies, where the ethnomusicologist and author of *Song from the Forest*, Louis Sarno, has been living since 1990. I had visited Sarno as well, on the last leg of my elephant reporting safari. There's nothing like the cascading polyphonic yodeling of Pygmies, their joyous blendings of three- and four-note segments of the minor pentatonic, of multiple pentatonics. It's been called the Uhr music, because it's the most primordial music, closest to the original melodic vocalizations humans started to make. Louis Sarno first heard it on the radio late at night in Amsterdam, where he was agonizing over an abstruse doctoral thesis involving higher math and post-Wittgensteinian deconstructionism, and he was so blown away that he dropped everything and cashed in all his chips and six months later arrived in Yandoumbe with a little suitcase and has been there ever since. Bernie said, "What the Pygmies are basically doing is karaoke with the sounds of the forest, and some of their scales have twenty intervals, so the idea that the human, mammal, and bird ear organizes sound in the twelve-note octave is simplistic, to put it mildly, like the idea that birdsong can be captured by musical notation, as Mathews [whose field book has a score for each species] thought he did in 1913."

"This is true," I said. "Even in a simple song, like the chickadee's 'chickaDEE chickaDEEdee,' I can figure out what the notes are, but I can't play or sing them the way a chickadee does and I never will. It's coming from a completely different place."

Subsequently, Bernie and I had an enlightening back-and-forth about the some of the projections he maintains academic bioacousticians are guilty of. "The octave ranges in the critter world are entirely dependent on the acoustic properties of the habitat in which the bio-phonies take place," he e-mailed. "Topography, forest density, climate, weather, and the density and diversity of the collective critter biopho-nies all play a role in determining what occurs pitch-wise. In fact, in some habitats there may be forty, fifty, or more insect, reptile, bird, or mammal pitches that define an octave. That is why groups like the Ba'Aka (CAR), or the Yanomami, Kaluli (Papua New Guinea), or the Jivaro (Amazon Basin), who mimic the voices of the forest around them, perform in what we academics call 'micro-tonal' scales. But that, too, is a misnomer since those aren't microtones to those groups. Nor is it music (they don't have a word for 'music' in their language. Neither do they have a word for musician, performer, or artist). It's just a natural connection to the vocal forest spirits around them and to which they show deference by singing and/or dancing along with the band."

Sitting now in his lab, Bernie, frequently interrupting our conversation excitedly to play me one of his fantastic recordings—"Wait'll you hear this!"—explains that we didn't just get our music from the birds, but our morality, such as it is: "If you listen to a dawn or twilight chorus in a rain forest, every animal gets his chance to sing and be heard, his moment to impress potential mates with his sincerity and virtuosity. There is an implicit understanding, okay, this is where you come in, the beginning of a social contract, cooperation even in competitive space. Everybody's individual rights are respected. And the order that they come in—first the insects, then the frogs, then the birds, and finally the mammals—is in evolutionary order, so the biophony is also teaching them about the structure of the creation, the ontology, biology. There are eighteen disciplines that the biophony teaches."

"Just like the waterhole in Zimbabwe," I say (I had told him about Johnny Rodrigues's video). "The animals that came to it had manners and consideration, polite civilized queue behavior."

Bernie recorded over fifteen thousand species and four thousand hours of wild soundscapes, half of which he says no longer exist be-cause of human encroachment and ecocide. "You turn a wetland into pasture or pave it over and you wipe out the biophony," he says. "Here's a recording of a beaver by colleagues in Minnesota, at a small remote lake after Fish and Wildlife blew up his dam and killed his mate and offspring. The male is swimming around looking for its mate. It's the saddest sound I've ever heard.

"Ever heard an anemone sing?" he goes on. "Are you sitting down?" (I'm sitting right next to him.) "I dropped a hydrophone down the middle of it. The tentacles are looking for something of nutritional value but don't find it so they expel the hydrophone. Ever hear ants sing 'Ant Misbehavin"? I dropped a little tiny lavalier mic into an anthill. This is the sound of ants stridulating, rubbing their legs on their abdomens.

"Here's two hungry baby vultures in a tree in Napo, Ecuador, using its hollow shell as a resonator to amplify their cries. These low roars are howler monkeys in Panama. One of the great sounds in the neotropical rain forest." (In my book *The Rivers Amazon*, I compare them to "wind rushing out of the portals of Hades.")

"Check this out: the sounds of thunderstorms on the equator, whose electronic energy is transmitted though the Earth's magnetic field to both poles, where they are picked up by radio receivers. Now listen to a Weddell seal in the Antarctic doing the same thing, and now a bearded seal in the Arctic ten thousand miles away—same thing. It's as though they're both imitating thunderstorms on the equator.

"The more humble we are about our contentions about the natural world," Bernie explains, "the more we are going to find out. You have to be open to things happening. That's the essence of scientific inquiry. You keep that avenue of curiosity open. I'm going to get smacked upside the head every which way by the academic bioacousticians because this book [*The Great Animal Orchestra*, which hadn't been published when we had this conversation] doesn't fit their modes. But don't say that. I don't want to give them an opening. I don't want to get into a food fight. I want to put it out there, and give it to individuals who are young and don't know enough not to know these things are not possible."

(In fact, the book's reviews were almost all raves, and it has even inspired a symphony.)

He gives me a copy of his CD, *Gorillas in the Mix*, his compositions performed entirely by animal sounds. One of the cuts is a samba called "Trout from Ipanema."

"Jobim [Antônio Carlos Jobim, the composer of "The Girl from Ipanema," of which Bernie's song is a rendering] loved it. We got to be pals," before Jobim's death, in 1994.

Bernie has been to Camp Leakey in Borneo, where Biruté Mary Galdikas did her research on the orangutans, and where I'm heading next. "Give her my regards, and crawl up the tower before sunrise so you can hear the gibbon duets, the males and females singing to each other. You're gonna love it."

This reporting safari had been incredibly productive in terms of expanding my knowledge base about animals. I had "gotten down," to various degrees, with a raven, marmosets, black vultures, lynx, an elephant, horses, dolphins, a bonobo. Of course there is an element of subjectivity in such connections, but consciousness can only be experienced and explained in terms of one's own personal consciousness. I now had a much better understanding of how to be in the presence of an animal and how to initiate interaction with it. And I had met some really interesting people. And the trip wasn't over.

There was one last stop, the pot of gold at the end of the rainbow: Borneo. I was going to meet Biruté Mary Galdikas and the orangutans she has devoted her life to and finally get to the world's third-largest rain forest, after the Amazon and Equatorial African ones that I had spent so much time in. It and a few places on mainland Malaysia have the oldest and most biodiverse forest of any kind on the planet. I had long wanted to meet the third of Louis Leakey's "angels," young women he sent to learn everything they could about the great apes and to organize their protection—Jane Goodall to the chimpanzees, Dian Fossey to the mountain gorillas, Galdikas to the orangutans. The very sound of the word *Borneo* was enough to generate a frisson of excitement as I headed west across the Pacific to Singapore and connected with my flight to Jakarta.

PART FOUR

VANISHING EDENS

First Trip to Borneo: With Dr. Galdikas
and Her Orangutans in Kalimantan

When I stopped to see Bubbles in Myrtle Beach, Doc Antle told me he had just gotten back from Borneo. He brought Dr. Galdikas some radio collars to track the sun bears who live up in the trees with the orangutans. Orangutan Foundation International, her organization, is one of the causes he supports. "Borneo is so beautiful and fabulous," he told me, "and it's so blatantly being raped and pillaged, it's heart wrenching. These gentle creatures are living on the last islands of forest. They're being ecoslaughtered by palm oil and logging. Biruté's very cool, very enlightened, almost an orangutan herself."

It was paleoanthropologist Louis Leakey's "eccentric" idea to send young women with no formal scientific training, and therefore no preconceptions, to study our closest primate relatives, the great apes. He picked three women who seemed to have a strong maternal instinct and nurturing capacity, reasoning, correctly, that they would also fight with their dying breath for the apes' survival. Galdikas compares the first of Leakey's "angels," the lovely, innocent Jane Goodall, to Dorothy in *The Wizard of Oz*, and the second, the darker, more complicated Dian Fossey, to Judy Garland in her 1995 book, *Reflections of Eden: My Years with the Orangutans of Borneo*, which I am blearily reading in the airport in Jakarta, waiting for the puddle jumper to Pangkalanbun, a town in Kalimantan, the southern, Indonesian two-thirds of Borneo. I'm supposed to find Dr. Galdikas at her orangutan care center in an indigenous Dayak village on the outskirts of Pangkalanbun, but I look up and there she is—I recognize her from her photos—a gray-haired woman with glasses and a sensitive, round Baltic face sitting in the next room with two young women. They're waiting for the same flight. So I go over to their table and say, "Dr. Galdikas, I presume."

They are returning to the care center after a week in Jakarta trying to resolve a major crisis. One of Biruté's companions is a high-powered businesswoman who has her own IT company in Boston. After going on one of Biruté's VIP tours, she became a passionate convert to the orangutan cause. She is helping straighten out the Orangutan Foundation's finances. The woman is beside herself, really distraught. She explains that there is a 250,000-acre property in Kalimantan called Rimba Raya, which was all set to become the first of the UN's REDD projects in the world. The acronym stands for Reducing Emissions from Deforestation and Forest Degradation. It's a scheme whereby industrial polluters in the rich countries can offset their carbon emissions by contributing to a "restoration concession," a tract of tropical forest like Rimba Raya that's left alone for twenty years. The trees can't be logged, so they can continue to grow and extract CO_2 out of the atmosphere and convert it to cellulose and thus help neutralize the CO_2 the polluters are pouring into the atmosphere. The polluters who sign on get "carbon credits" that they can sell to other polluters at any stage, whenever they want out. This ingenious protocol, launched in 2008 at the United Nations' Climate Change Conference in Poland, is not a perfect solution, but at least it's something, and there are collateral benefits: it conserves biodiversity, buying twenty years for the living things in the forest you are protecting. And in the case of Rimba Raya, it was going to provide a home for 100 of the 350 orangutans confiscated from pet owners and loggers, orphans picked up by somebody who found them, abandoned pets who have grown too big, those fleeing the flames and smoke of the incineration of their trees, found starving from the loss of their wild food sources, who are waiting in cages in the care center to be returned to the forest. "But there's hardly any forest left for them to be released in," the woman told me.

Up until this point, everything was looking good. A group of green American businessmen called Infinite Earth spent a million dollars doing the necessary verification and validation of the Rimba Raya property, Russia's Gazprom was on board, and so were the two ministers of forestry in Jakarta who came and went while the lengthy process of certification proceeded. But now a third minister had come in and granted one-tenth of the property as a concession to an oil-palm company, which was going to clear and torch it and plant rows of oil-palm trees. And this was the most intact forest, the part where Biruté was planning to release the hundred orangutans. Most of Rimba Raya had been cut and burned and abandoned and was in the early stages of reversion to forest—no good for orangutans.

Furthermore, these pristine twenty-five thousand acres of Rimba Raya were peat forest. The peat was twenty feet deep, and after the vegetation was torched, unless it was drenched by rain, it would burn and smolder for months, releasing huge amounts of CO_2. This was what happened in the fall of 1997, when much of Kalimantan's peat forest, which had been cleared for rice and palm oil, was burning out of control, and much of Southeast Asia was blanketed in thick black smoke. Some of the acrid fumes had drifted all the way to Japan and burned our eyes in Kyoto, where the UN conference on climate change, which I was covering for *Vanity Fair*, was taking place. And in 2015 the peat fires in Indonesia, including Kalimantan, will be so bad again that their smoke will be visible from space and their president will implore international assistance in putting them out. Thousands of orangutans will die of starvation or smoke inhalation or be killed by villagers whose plantations they have invaded.

The three women were trying to get this concession reversed, or at least transferred to some other part of the property, but the oil-palm company wasn't interested because it wanted the money from the trees. There was a lot of valuable timber in there. It was a total disaster. The whole REDD program in Indonesia could collapse if this went through. Norway, its main backer, would pull out if its flagship project was made such a mockery of.

After years of dealing with Indonesian bureaucrats, Dr. Galdikas knew that getting action from them is a long, drawn-out process of ceremonial cordiality and consensus building. You don't get in their faces or become confrontational—something that Dian Fossey didn't abide by in Rwanda, which is probably what got her killed. So she wasn't as upset about the week with nothing to show for it as the woman from Boston.

Dr. Galdikas had no illusions about what a scurvy lot we humans are, or can be, or how daunting the battle to save the orangutans, and all the world's remaining free-ranging animals, is. But this only made her all the more determined to do everything she could for these extraordinary, innocent creatures that she had been charged to learn about and protect by Leakey years ago, and whose right to exist she had come to feel she had been put on Earth to defend.

I studied her as she sat there, relaxing and enjoying a little downtime before the next energy-demanding activity. She was reserved but cozy and earthy with a mischievous twinkle and, I knew from reading her book, a sophisticated, inquisitive mind. And she on her part was quietly sussing me out, having not fared well at the hand of other writers. So Dr. Galdikas needed to ascertain what my motives were. Not until the third day of my six-day visit did she declare, "I'm glad to see you are good-natured." From then on, we were fast friends, sharing stories about mutual acquaintances in the small, treacherous arena of primate behavior. She calls me Pak Alex. *Pak* is a respectful title for an older man, like the Brazilian Portuguese *seu*, or the Swahili *mzei*. I call her Dr. Biruté, or Dr. B for short. Dr. Galdikas is too formal.

The Rimba Raya crisis is only one of the million things Dr. B has to contend with before heading back to Vancouver to teach her fall primatology course at Simon Fraser University, as she has been doing for twenty years. On top of the list is to make sure there is money to feed the 350 orangutans in the care center and two overflow facilities for the next three months. Her garage is already full of eleven thousand dollars' worth of durian fruits, which will not last even two weeks. Two thirds of OFI's annual budget of $600,000 is spent on durian and other forest fruits. So she is running around and scraping up bundles of *rupiah*, the local currency, for the umpteenth time. Keeping up such a frenetic pace is obviously not something she is going to be able to do forever, and thankfully she has young female interns helping out at the center. They look up to her as if she were Mother Teresa. Janie

Dubman, the other woman with Dr. B at the airport, is a super-bright twenty-two-year-old who speaks Russian, Hebrew, English, and Indonesian, a third-time intern, and one of her students. "No one has more tenacity than Dr. Galdikas," she tells me. "I've never met somebody with such a pure single-minded mission. It's all driven by orangutan welfare and forest protection. She drives herself to the brink of exhaustion. She's gotten sick so many times. She tries every approach there is. It sounds cheesy, but her heart is pure. She's a mentor to all of us and my favorite kind of leader because she leads by example, which is why we all are involved and committed to taking some of the burden off her shoulders."

On the first afternoon of my visit, we go up to Camp Leakey: myself, Dr. B, Janie, and an older research assistant who is collecting samples of orangutan dung to get an idea of family relatedness through their DNA. The four of us drive down to the Port of Kumai on the Java Sea, and take a little speedboat across the bay and up the Sekonyer River, which is lined with impenetrable nipa palm, which gives way to equally impenetrable screw palm as the water gets fresher. Dr. B points to three proboscis monkeys sitting up in a tree, with big, floppy Walter Matthau schnozzes, gazing out on the 150-foot-wide river. There are only three thousand of them left in the wild. We pass several more groups and resting troops of smaller, gray, long-tailed macaques, also known as crab-eating macaques. We keep passing tourist boats. Forty-three of them ply the Sekonyer. The tourists sleep and dine in the boats that take them up to Camp Leakey to see the orangutans. Ecotourism arrived, for better or worse, in the late nineties.

We pull up to the staff dock, and as we walk down a long boardwalk through a peat swamp we are greeted by some of Dr. B's oldest orangutan friends, who have somehow picked up from the jungle tom-tom that she has arrived. First Mooch and Maio, then Peta and Petra, and Akmad and Atlas. Biruté and Akmad go back forty years. We reach the camp and there is a welcoming committee of several dozen more, as well as two habituated Bornean bearded pigs.

Dr. B has brought several gunny sacks of durian fruit, which she distributes, and soon the animals are all pigging out. Dr. B and her collaborators have an ongoing project to identify the different things the orangutans eat, and so far the list is up to four hundred. Borneo's forests are the richest on Earth, with some fifteen thousand species of higher plants and three thousand species of trees, and life for its fifty thousand or so orangutans is a constant search for their next meal. Most orangutan behavior, Janie explains, is food-driven. This is because the trees that are in fruit at any given time in the forest are few and far between. The sparsity of food sources limits their ability to be in large groups and is thus one of the main determinants of their semisolitary social behavior. They have temporary gatherings at a tree that is in fruit, adult males and females form consortships for a few months, and mothers and children stay together, the kids clinging to them for seven or eight years, longer than any other primate—more like elephants. The females stay in a home range that is pretty much the same as their mother's, while the males are nomadic and wander all over the forest, spending 90 percent of their time alone. They sit for hours in the crowns of the tallest trees, "contemplating the universe," as Dr. B puts it, or "conserving energy," in Janie's more biological interpretation, scanning the forest canopy for trees in fruit or with newly flushed leaves, watching the movements of hornbills (where they mob means there is something to eat), tracing the trails of other orangutans—the fresh swaths they have cut through the treetops—also meaning they have found food.

"Orangutans are fantastic botanists," says Janie, and they have an encyclopedic memory of when and where a particular tree will be in fruit. They treat each other with plants that humans use medicinally. For instance, they chew leaves in the genus *Commelina* into a soapy foam that acts as an anti-inflammatory and muscle relaxant. Dr. B contends that they are capable of abstraction, that they do, in fact, see the forest for the trees, because they have a whole map of it in their minds. When they're up there in the top of some emergent dipterocarp—a family of pantropical trees of which Borneo is the world center of diversity, with 380 of the 500 species—they're plotting their movements for the next few days, weighing a host of factors. (Dipterocarps are so named because they have fruits the size of a golf ball that have two six-inch plumes shooting out from either side to cushion their fall from the canopy.)

According to local belief, orangutans are people (*orang hutan* means "people of the forest" in Indonesian) who were deprived of language and banished for blasphemy. But to Biruté they are "the children of

Eden." They were never thrown out of the garden for eating the for-
bidden fruit; they have no knowledge of good and evil so they aren't
capable of doing evil, unlike humans.

The forest around Camp Leakey, which we spend several hours wandering in, is certainly Eden-like, a paradisal emerald forest, although
the Dayak, the local indigenous people (*Dayak* is a catchall term, like
Indians, for Borneo's two hundred–some ethnic groups, which is obsolete in Sarawak, Brunei, and Sabah but still used in Kalimantan), see it
as full of malevolent spirits, like the *gaip*, little people who live in the
deepest, darkest part of the forest and who, if you cut down their homes
or move near their settlements, get angry and unleash terrible diseases.
Only children can see the *gaip*. They are invisible to adults. A few days
later we will walk with an old Dayak man through a 7,500-acre forest
that he is selling to Dr. B for $100 an acre. He could have sold it to the
oil-palm or mangosteen growers for a lot more, but they would have cut
it down, and he didn't want to incur the wrath of the *gaip*.

The forest we are now in is dead quiet except for the fantastic virtuosic
arias of a straw-headed bulbul who is filling the Pavarotti niche. The
evening concert, in which all the animals join in, has not begun. I make
a lame attempt to answer the bulbul's elaborate riffs with my guitalele,
and it falls silent, like the thrush in our back alley in Montreal I had a
brief exchange with. Who is that? Definitely not one of us. Not worthy
of having a sing-off with. What Dr. B admires most about orangutans,
she tells me as we sit on a log, is that "they're self-contained universes. I
compare them to God. If an orangutan never saw another, it wouldn't
bother them."

None of this aloofness is on display back at Camp Leakey, however.
As I am walking down the path toward camp, a female no higher than
my hip takes my hand and pulls on it so hard I have to lean the other
way to keep my balance. Orangutans are really strong, with Popeye
arms reaching below their knees. We all hang out together on the porch,
forgetting that there is any barrier between us. Orangutans make many
of the same facial expressions we do and they love to mug. The lower
halves of their faces are rubbery with big U-shaped mouths, and they're
incredible mimics. The ones near me are looking searchingly into my
eyes and aping every lip shift.

Others are hanging around in the trees and looking down on us, swinging effortlessly on branches and vines, putting on a nonstop show of breathtaking gymnastics and fluidity without giving it a second thought. Their feet are more like hands. It's kind of like they're cartwheeling and penduluming through the trees, which they can move through faster than we can walk on the ground. They're too heavy to make the sixty-foot leaps from tree to tree that gibbons, whose dawn choruses I am dying to hear, do. Why only orangutans, of all the apes, have orange-reddish hair, is not known.

First Encounter with the Devastation

The next day we drive out to Rimba Raya, the sabotaged REDD project, to see how the thirty orangutans she has already released in anticipation of its approval, before this third minister came in, are doing. It's on the northern border of the 1,174-square-mile Tanjung Puting National Park and UNESCO Biosphere Reserve that Camp Leakey is in the southernmost part of. So we have to drive around it.

The forest (as I described at the beginning of this book) is completely gone. Nothing but row after row of oil palm all the way to a hazy blue ridgeline of mountains far in the distance. "What a horror show," I say to Dr. B. "I had no idea this was happening."

The oil-palm tree, *Elaeis guineensis*, is native to West Africa. It began to be planted extensively in Malaysia in the 1960s and '70s. The newly independent country needed something to get its economy going, and the government in Kuala Lumpur decided it should be its rain forest hardwoods and palm oil. Today 1.5 million hectares of Sabah (one hectare is 2.47 acres) are planted with palm oil. Sarawak has 1 million, which it plans to double. Indonesia started more slowly, but by the eighties it surpassed Malaysia. Today it is the world's biggest producer and consumer of the commodity, providing half the world's supply. By the end of 2010, palm plantations covered more than 3.1 million hectares of Kalimantan, out of a total of about 10.8 million hectares in Indonesia, and another 4 million hectares are slated to be cleared and planted, or are already being converted, to supply the growing market for biodiesel fuel. Indonesia's palm oil production increased 213-fold from 157,000 tonnes in 1965 to 33.5 million tonnes in 2014. Ninety percent of the lowland Borneo rain forest, the oldest, most species-rich and widespread type of forest on the island, is gone, 50 percent of the island's forest cover. The deforestation rate in Borneo since 1980 has been, according to Mongabay.com, unparalleled in human history, much greater than that of the Amazon, with 60 to 240 cubic meters of wood being harvested per hectare in Borneo in the 1980s and '90s versus 23 cubic meters per hectare in the Amazon.

But so under the radar is the devastation the logging and palm-oil industries have done and are continuing to do in Southeast Asia that when I wrote a piece for *Vanity Fair* in 2007 called "A Day in the Life of a Modern Consumer," an attempt to lay out the often faraway impacts of everything we consume, I wasn't even aware of the impact of palm oil, or of the hundreds of products that contain it. From my toothpaste, to my bar soap, shampoo, and shaving cream, before I even stepped out the door I was multiply compromised in the annihilation that is now off to our left. As we travel north at a good clip for an hour and a half, for at least fifty miles, to our left, and twenty or thirty miles in, it is nothing but palm trees, row after row of them flickering by.

The Demonic Male

We turn right and drive east along the northern boundary of the park on the road to the release station in Rimba Raya that was built for the 2011 IMAX film *Born to Be Wild*, shot here and at Daphne Sheldrick's elephant orphanage in Nairobi. A strange slouching bohemian hipster orangutan emerges from the tall bracken and stands in the middle of the road in front of us, forcing us to stop. It is Congo, a male about fifteen years old who is running from Eddie, a huge wild male "cheek pad" who has discovered that there is food at the station and has been throwing his weight around.

When a male orangutan reaches sexual maturity, if the conditions are right—that is, there isn't a big cheek pad already in the vicinity—hairless black flanges sprout along his jowls, making him more fearsome, and he bloats up like a two-hundred-pound sumo wrestler. Nobody wants to tangle with a cheek pad, and when one of them lets out its blood-curdling long call, which can be heard for several miles, the lesser males make themselves scarce, and the females wait apprehensively to see which of them he is going to forcibly copulate with. The act is considered a mark of status for the female, according to Dr. Galdikas. I had a harrowing incident at the care center with a gigantic cheek pad named Roy, who was sitting alone in his cage as still as a rock, and formidable, apparently deep in a meditative state, like a giant Buddha statue. I went over to his cage to say hello, and when I got within two feet of the bars, his right arm shot out and before I knew it I was pinned and completely helpless. He could have snapped off one of my arms or crushed my skull with his teeth, but instead with his left hand he tore the buttons off my shirt and then from my left wrist the small multicolored glass-beaded bracelet a Babendjele Pygmy had given me the previous year. Two of the workers came running with a high-powered hose and drove him back to the far corner of the cage like a civil rights protester in Birmingham in 1963.

Roy was in all probability just acting the way a cheek pad is supposed to. He was showing the dozens of other orangutans who witnessed his cunning move from their cages that even behind bars, he was still the boss. Dr. B doesn't know Roy's backstory but suspects he wasn't a captive for very long before he was brought to the center. Still, I have trouble feeling warm and fuzzy about these cheek pads. It is true that having someone who is so huge and brutal that no one will fight with him is adaptive in the sense that it prevents actual combat, which is maladaptive for both sides, and prevents the bloody warfare, mutilation, and cannibalization that chimps are into. But the cheek pads set a terrible example. They are the epitome, the prototype, of domination by superior force, of the ruthless resource-gathering drive that gives rise to what the primatologist Richard Wrangham has called "the demonic male," that in our species is responsible for war and sadistic dictators, savage capitalists and the ongoing devastation of the planet. So I'm not a fan. Every society is compromised in some way, and the compromise in orangutan society is that it has these scary dudes.

In 2015 I went back to see the mountain gorillas in Volcanoes National Park (before Rwanda's switch to English, it was the Parc National des Volcans) with my twenty-year-old son, Zachary, and his girlfriend. We, and another human family of five, and our two guides, were standing right above a dominant silverback with his females and their children. He was standing in the Buddha pose, looking off inscrutably into the distance, which, having had the experience with Roy, I was not completely buying. Suddenly he let out a blood-curdling roar and bolted up to a nearby knoll on all fours, with a speed and power we would have been unable to flee. Apparently he heard something threatening, like a buffalo. His family followed right after him, and we followed it. There was nothing. Maybe he just did it to scare us, to remind us that we were only visiting with his family because he was allowing us to. So it's not just orangutan cheek pads who use this ruse, although the silverback seemed to be making a show of strength to protect his family, and not demonstrating demonic machismo.

Dinner with Kristin

A greeting party of about thirty orangutans has materialized from the forest and assembled in the clearing by the time we pull up to the release station. "There you go," Dr. B says. "The planet of the apes. We're getting a royal welcome here." They're an incredible cast of characters, each with a different posture and demeanor. Some come up and greet Dr. B, while others hang on the periphery, watching.

We all proceed to a clearing one hundred yards from the steward's shack where there is a platform that all the orangutans climb up and sit on, and Biruté hands out the durian fruit. But just as they are about to dig in, Eddie, who has been following us in the treetops, comes down and climbs up the rear of the platform, and the others all hastily bolt off it.

"If you want intelligence, Kristin's your girl," Dr. B says, pointing to an orangutan who is peering through the cracks in the board siding of the steward's shack when we get back to the clearing. Dinner of noodle soup has been prepared in the kitchen inside. The smell is making me hungry. As we six humans are all sitting on the floor and passing our bowls to the cook to fill, Kristin quietly unlatches the door to the shack from inside with a stick and sits down with us. She tucks her napkin under her chin, picks up her spoon and delicately, with the most exquisite table manners, spoons up the soup in her bowl without slurping even once. As we are taking part in the breaking of bread together and chatting away, as humans do, Kristin gives each speaker her undivided attention, as if, like Queen Elizabeth, she is deeply interested in what the person has to say. Then, when her meal is over and she has had enough of this curious ritual, she removes her napkin, folds it, places it beside her empty bowl and puts her spoon on it, gets up, lets herself out, and ever so softly relatches the door from the outside with the stick again.

"Nobody taught her to do this," Biruté assures me. "She picked it up all by herself."

These Indonesian apes never cease to amaze with their ability to pick up on what their human fellow-primates are doing. The latest thing is that orangutans in North American zoos are being given iPads so they can communicate with each other in different zoos during the cold winter months when they can't go outside, and they've taken to the marvelous gadgets like ducks to water. They use them to play memory and painting games, even to Skype with other orangutans. But watching nature videos is their favorite.

We emerge from the shack as the sun is setting. All the orangutans have gone, melted back into the forest, and are making their nests for the night. Each night each one makes a new nest in a different tree, and sleeps alone in it. The nest making is instinctive. Several of those released here had spent their life in captivity and started to build nests from their very first day in the forest.

Orangutans' semisolitariness is deeply ingrained, like the aloofness of cats, I reflect, while we humans are so hypersocial. We need each other's approval, we need to constantly reassure each other we're on the same side. Supposedly we need three hours of social interaction to maintain a healthy profile, so we spend all this time and energy building social capital, but for what? It's all bullshit, you realize when you're old and no longer in the game. Bullshit the orangutans don't have. No wonder Dr. B admires them so much.

"So that's what the orangutans have to teach us," I say to her. "We're alone, and it's okay."

And Dr. B says, "But if we lose the animals, it's going to be very lonely."

The Oil-Palm Growers

While I was in Pangkalanbun, there was a convention of oil-palm growers at the hotel where I was staying. One was a Chinese man from Singapore about my age, elegant and aristocratic in a blue blazer with gold buttons. "I don't understand why people care about these orangutans," he told me. He reminded me of a rich Republican back home railing against the animal lovers and the tree huggers. I told him about Kristin unlatching the door at Dr. Galdikas's research station and joining us for dinner, her perfect manners, how she gave each of us her undivided attention whenever we said something, like the Queen. I didn't give him an opening to get going on the backward tribals who need to be brought into the modern world and given the blessings of progress—in return for their land and its trees, of course.

Another, more caring grower from Singapore, in his early thirties— also named Alex—said the big money was in the hardwoods in the rain forest. "And you can't lecture us about cutting down our forest, because that's what you did, and how America got where it is. And after the forest is gone, you have to plant something, and the crop that gives the best return for the longest time, the most sustainable commodity, is the oil-palm tree, which lives for twenty years and can be replanted. If this was the Amazon, it would be pasture for beef cattle or planted with soybeans, but neither of them is as efficient. These trees produce up to ten times the amount of oil per hectare in comparison with other vegetable oil crops such as soy and canola.

"But I have mixed feelings about what the removal of the forest is doing to the orangutans," Alex confided. "Some of the palm growers are trying to help the orangutans by leaving corridors of rain forest for them. We left a pathway through our estate in Sabah for the pygmy elephants and we didn't do anything to control them, and eventually they did damage to some of the palms. Sabah is more conscious of the need to leave intact forest habitat for its wildlife than Indonesia or Sarawak. In 2004 we started a roundtable for sustainable palm oil, the RSPO. Its members are committed to doing it right, to leave wildlife corridors and strips of forest along the river and not to slash and burn the peat forests. Peat fires, once they get going, burn for months and are impossible to put out. But only 6 percent of the industry, the big multinationals who are image conscious and can afford to give up the land, have been certified as sustainable by RSPO. And not all of them. Unilever, the world's biggest consumer of palm oil, Nestlé, and Kraft have canceled their contracts with Sinar Mas, the biggest palm oil producer in Indonesia, because it is still clearing and burning peat forest and ignoring the other sustainability criteria even though it's a member of the RSPO."

Alex was a perfectly decent guy, providing for his family. Palm oil is where the action is in his part of the world. Not everybody in the industry can be demonized. Alex made me think about the question of individual responsibility versus the system that gives us all these great things—shampoo, lipstick, and the hundreds of other products most of us aren't even aware contain palm oil—the capitalist, earth-killing system that we need to change.

The Year of the Animists

After that trip, I had a much better understanding of the wavelength animals are on. Adam's Wall, the barrier between us and the other species, kind of just wasn't there anymore. Walking down the sidewalk of our block in Montreal one morning, I pass a woman with a dog on a leash, and the dog licks the back of my hand, an interspecies high five like the street elephant in Thailand the year before who ran the moist tip of his trunk over my arm. I have met so many different and wonderful new animals and people, it has changed me. I am much more alive to the communications that are going on between all of us transitional characters, particularly to the biophony.

If 2010–2012 brought me in contact with a lot of different animals and animal people, 2013 was shaping up to be the year of the hunter-gatherers and would enable me to pull together my thoughts about the indigenous people I'd been visiting for forty years: their fascinating cosmologies and animistic belief systems; the horrors they have experienced as their ecosystems have been destroyed by loggers, miners, hydro dams, poachers; the shattering of the equilibrium that took centuries or millennia to establish with their ecosystems and their fellow-creatures; and their struggles to keep their cultures and way of life alive. In February I had dinner in New York City with the Brazilian photographer Sebastião

Salgado to discuss the possibility of our doing a story together for *Vanity Fair*. Salgado had spent ten years going, like me, to the last vanishing Edens, and celebrating and documenting the lives of their inhabitants, human and animal, with powerful black-and-white images. A lavish coffee-table book with his pictures, *Genesis*, was just coming out, and magnificent exhibitions of them were opening in Paris, Rio, then the rest of the world.

Salgado had gone to thirty-two places and spent months in each. He had been to the San (Bushmen) of the Kalahari Desert, as I had, in 2009. It was like discovering that you were seventy-five thousand years old, he told me. I knew exactly what he meant, and told him of my visit with the family of N!xau, the star of *The Gods Must Be Crazy*. We went out into the desert and they showed me how they get everything they need that day in four hours. They dug up juicy water cucumbers buried in the sand, and showed me the beetle grub they make their arrow poison from, they started a fire with two sticks and a ball of zebra dung in less than a minute. The San have the greatest amount of leisure time of any society, and they don't have mortgages, bosses, or money problems, which makes you wonder how much the progress of Western civilization has actually been progress. In the movie a Coke bottle falls out of the sky and N!xau's band doesn't know what to make of it. At first they think it's a miraculous gift from heaven (in fact some white guy chucked it out of the window of his bush plane). The Coke bottle, they discover, has all kinds of uses. You can make fire with it, use it as a magnifying glass, blow it, pulverize tubers with it. But it soon leads to discord. The band members, who have never had any problems with each other, begin to fight over it, and finally they collectively decide they were better off before it fell out of the sky so inexplicably, and that it has to go. N!xau takes it to the edge of a cliff, several days' walk, to the edge of their known world, and flings it off, out of their lives. It's a beautiful metaphor for the downside of "progress" and the consumer culture.

That night I danced around a bonfire with the men, while the women sat around it singing in cascading polyphonies while clapping complicated cross-rhythms. All of us dancers had seed rattles around our ankles, and as we trudged around the fire, I realized that although I had danced with many indigenous people, this was something much deeper and older. The San are the people who have been living longest in the same place, maybe seventy-five thousand years, longer than anybody anywhere, and they (the three hundred or so who are still living traditionally; the other eighty thousand work as ranch hands and at other menial jobs in the modern culture) have been doing this dance three or four times a week, so they really have it down. After maybe fifteen minutes, I started to go into a trance, which all the other dancers were in. Several of the men were shamans who dance themselves into theriomorphs, half human, half animal, which there are ancient pictographs of in caves, made by their ancestors.

On this night, in one of the emptiest quarters in Africa, we were all dancing or sitting around the fire together in the desert, under a sky blazing with stars. There was no dyadic us-them "now the natives are going to dance for us"; they were doing their dance, sharing with us what they did. No matter that we were at this luxurious safari tent camp, after a while there was no difference between us, the rich white tourists, and these San who were off the grid, living in another time and world. We were united by the basic fact that we were all going to die. "That's just how I felt, Sebastião, as if I discovered that I was seventy-five thousand years old," I told him.

A few months after our meeting in New York, I got a call from Salgado inviting me to come with him to Brazil to see what we could do for an indigenous people called the Awá, who live in easternmost Amazonia, in the state of Maranhão. Some fifty of them are still uncontacted nomadic hunter-gatherers, with no fixed villages or crops, living on what they hunt with bows and arrows and the fruits and nuts and honey they collect, throwing up palm-thatch lean-tos and moving on every few days. Over the years, fifteen hundred families of squatters have moved into their *terra indígena*, a third of their forest has been cut, and loggers are within a few miles of one of the uncontacted bands. The Awá are in their endgame, between the loggers who are working for some of Maranhão's most powerful families, and the squatters who have their blessing. Survival International has designated them the most endangered people on Earth.

The Awá, we will discover, have a really interesting cosmology and social system. Here's the beginning of "The Last of Eden," the piece I wrote about them:

> The welcoming committee comes down from the village. Three of the men have yellow crowns of toucan feathers, red toucan-feather bracelets on their upper arms, and red toucan down dabbed on the tip of their foreskins, which are tied up with string. They are carrying beautifully made longbows and arrows that come to their shoulders. The tallest man is called Piraí. He sits on one of the benches behind the Brazilian National Indian Foundation's [FUNAI's] post of Juriti, where I am staying, and his wife, Pakoyaí, in a skirt of finely woven tucum palm, sits next to him. Their son Iuwí is to his right, and in the background is his father, Pirahá, who is also married to Iuwí's sister, so Pirahá is both Iuwí's grandfather and his brother-in-law. Pirahá has a big smile, which I recognize is the smirk of someone with a sense of the absurd, who appreciates the delicious ironies, the constant outrageous surprises of existence, as people tend to do at the end of their lives. He is listening to a bird in the nearby forest that is singing in triplets. Emaciated dogs, little brown bags of bones, are snoozing and rolling in the dust. A rooster is prancing on the path for the benefit of a dozen hens and lesser males. Our gathering, on one of the last islands of intact rain forest in the eastern Amazon, is taking place in the context of an entire eco-system. All these communications and interactions are going on that our contingent from the modern world is dead to.
>
> Piraí starts to speak in Portuguese, his voice full of gravitas and emotion. "We are Awá," he says. "We don't succeed in living with chickens and cows. We don't want to live in cities. We want to live here. We have much courage, but we need you close to us. The Ka'apor and Guajajara"—neighboring tribes the Awá have testy relationships with—"are selling their wood to the whites. We don't want their money and their motorcycles. We don't want anything from the whites but to live as we live and be who we are. We just want to be Awá."
>
> Then Iuwí gives an impassioned speech in Awá, which none of us understand, but his words have such conviction and pride they

bring tears to my eyes. Two courageous Awá men, father and son, in their prime—there are not many others here in their demographic, nowhere near enough to take on the *madeireiros*, the loggers who are killing their trees and their animals and are now within a few miles of here, and the thousands of other *invasores* who have illegally settled on their land and converted a third of their forest to pasture. I think of all the speeches like this given by brave natives in the Americas over the last 500 years, who were trying to save their people and way of life and world but were unable to stop the inevitable, brutal advance of the conqueror and his "progress," and how this is probably what is going to happen here, to this remnant tribe in its endgame.

Uirá Garcia, an anthropologist who speaks Awá and spent thirteen months here researching their hunting, kinship, and cosmology, has flown up from São Paulo to help us understand them. "The forest is alive for the Awá," he explains. "They know exactly where they are at all times. Everywhere there is a story. 'This is where I killed a *paca*.' 'This is the tree I found honey in.'" He shows me a map of their trails that he made with some of the hunters. There are dozens, each with a different purpose. Some are only used seasonally. One goes to a place two days away where there are many *cupuaçu* trees. They take it only when the *cupuaçu* is in fruit.

Uirá shares what he has learned about the Awá's extraordinary take on their forest universe, the intricate web of correspondences and reciprocities they have with the plants and animals. "Every Awá is named for a plant or animal, with whom he has a special relationship for the rest of his life," he says. "Every species of tree has an animal that is its owner. The *araras*, parrots, are owners of the araucaria trees. The *guaribas*, the howlers, are the owners of the *uwariwa* trees. The other animals that eat the fruits of these trees have to ask permission of the parrots and the howlers, and the whole forest is structured this way. There is an underworld of ex-humans—ancestors of their enemies, the Guajajara, who fell through since-covered holes and are still living—and a heaven with magnificent beings called the Karawara, who come down to Earth to hunt and get water and honey. With the game disappearing, there will be a cosmic famine, because it won't be the end of just the Awá but the Karawara too. The end of the forest will be the end of the cosmos. There will be a famine on Earth and in heaven."

It's so important to preserve these stories, these cosmologies, these peoples and their connections to their forest, I think for the umpteenth time, because when they are gone, the human family loses out as yet another thread, another set of connections, that binds us to the Earth and the astonishing profusion of life on it, is cut. Like undiscovered species going extinct—we don't even know what we're losing. And each of these locally evolved mythologies and belief systems has their own logic and beauty; when you are in the environment that inspired them, they ring completely true.

The Awá are most afraid of the ghosts of the dead—the bad part of you that doesn't go to heaven, the anger that you have to have to be able to hunt and kill your brothers and sisters, the animals—who are drifting around in the forest and making otherwise unexplainable noises and are responsible for all illness, misfortune, and death.

There are sixty-six other known uncontacted groups in the Brazilian Amazon, and another thirty or so suspected ones. Two are still fully nomadic hunter-gatherers, living, like the Awá, the way people have lived for most of human history, for all but the last ten thousand years. Most of the people who have ever lived, some thirty billion of us, were nameless hunter-gatherers whose way of life and belief systems died with them. So these last ones are really precious. And yet the modern world, which has destroyed their cultures and taken their land, seems to care little about them. We care more about the wildlife in these last Edens. The World Wildlife Fund has six million members, and Survival International has only 150,000. How can this be? Preserving indigenous cultures and making people care about them is a more complicated business, because we still want their land and resources, and because the indigenous people themselves are increasingly ambivalent about the modern world, where to draw the line. One of the Awá women, who had been to FUNAI's health clinic in Imperatriz, the second-largest city in Maranhão, confessed that if she could live in the city and have a television and a refrigerator and a washing machine, she would do it in a flash.

Back to Borneo

Salgado's and my piece shined an international spotlight on the plight of the Awá, and put pressure on the Brazilian Ministry of Justice to finally take action. Early in 2014 they sent soldiers and military police to evict the squatters in their *terra indígena* and to bust the loggers, a move that it had been putting off for years.

Since the summer before, when I got back in touch with Davie, I had been thinking about an adventure we could go on together. In the fall I saw the horror show in Kalimantan, which almost nobody in the West knows or cares about, even though it's driven by our and Asia's consumption of palm oil, so Borneo was uppermost on my mind. Most of the remaining forest is in the mountainous heart of the island, where there are still some Penan who live in raised huts with palm-thatch roofs in the forest and hunt with blowguns and poison darts and move every couple of months (so they are not fully nomadic, but seminomadic) and have some interesting similarities with the Awá, some amazing convergences, considering they live halfway around the world from each other.

I have Eric Hansen's 1988 *Stranger in the Forest*, a jungle-adventure classic about his walking 2,300 miles through the heart of Borneo and back, with the help of local Penan, and Wade Davis, Ian Mackenzie, and Shane Kennedy's 1995 *Nomads of the Dawn*, which portrays them as gentle forest people, like most of the hunter-gatherers I have known, from Pygmies to Bushmen. The expert on the Penan is Ian Mackenzie. A linguist and ethnologist in his early sixties, he has spent some forty seasons among them. He speaks their language and has compiled the only dictionary of it and has collected their *suket*, the myths that explain their multitiered cosmology, which only a few of the elders remember; and has documented their names for 1,500 different trees, each with its associated spirit (usually of the same name). Mackenzie, whom I will meet in 2014, after hours of long talks on the phone, before and after our Sarawak safari, lives in Vancouver, in a rambling Edwardian house full of artifacts from Borneo and Papua New Guinea. His library is lined with old leather-bound volumes, mostly history, exploration, and natural science, including a 1778 edition of Diderot's *Encyclopédie*—the sort of books I have inherited from my great-uncle Avinoff. Mackenzie reminds me of him. In our many long talks, he will generously share his wealth of knowledge, even though he is writing his own book on the Penan or, rather, helping an elder named Galang write his memoirs.

"I first arrived in Sarawak in 1991 at the tail end of a trip to West Papua, where I had been clandestinely filming a documentary about the ethnocide that came with the Indonesian occupation," he tells me. "I realized that the Penans were suffering a similar fate. After a field trip that resulted in our book [*Nomads of the Dawn*] illustrating their material culture, my attention turned to their language and spiritual heritage. There was little good data on their culture, which had already suffered a mortal blow at the hands of the missionaries. There was no time to lose. It took me three years until my Penan was good enough to start looking for people who could tell me the old *suket*. I made the rounds of the remaining nomadic bands, but failed to find an informant. People in the West often believe that indigenous people are uniformly wise. In fact they're just like us: only a minority are intelligent and well informed. Besides, the missionaries had anathematized the old beliefs, so most people had willfully forgotten them. After six years I came to a group I'd never visited. It was a traditional encampment, and only on the following day did I learn they were tending rice fields nearby. There I met Galang, who, though nominally Christian, knew all the myths, and after some years trusted me enough to disclose the secrets of their cosmos, which contains seven or eight different worlds. Today, I am almost certain he is the last good Penan informant." So Mackenzie started working with Galang, and after many trips to his village and multiple months of taking down dictation, a four-volume autobiography has materialized. The first volume is now translated and ready to be submitted to publishers.

I find out about another seminomadic group—there are only three left, and none who are fully nomadic anymore, like the uncontacted Awá—we can camp with for ten days, and learn about their world and how they see things. A logging company has a concession to cut the big commercial trees in their forest, and their backs are to the wall. I manage to convince *Smithsonian Magazine* that people need to know what's happening in Borneo, because we're all implicated, and get them to hire my friend, award-winning photographer Cédric Houin, to take the pictures. The Penan are in Sarawak, and Cédric will be in Sabah, the other, smaller Malaysian state on Borneo, in the northeastern corner, separated from Sarawak by the tiny sliver of Brunei, shooting pictures for a French NGO, so all he has to do is fly over.

The Team Assembles in Miri

In the morning Davie and I check out of the no-frills motel outside Kuala Lumpur and fly down over the South China Sea to Miri, the second-largest city in Sarawak, a seething port of three hundred thousand. Cédric, or Varial, as he calls himself, meets us at the airport. Varial is his artistic name, the French term for some tricky skateboard maneuver. Varial skateboards everywhere in Montreal. He is also a passionate paraglider and is planning to sail down from the Andes to the *selva* of Ecuador with *Mami Wata*, Mother Earth to the indigenous forest people, painted on his wings, and to film the whole thing. A crazy idea but a beautiful one. Varial came from Paris fifteen years ago, the same time we fetched up there from upstate New York. He has given up a lucrative career doing fashion and commercial shoots and is devoting himself to documenting indigenous people and their fast-disappearing cultures, so it was only natural that we came into contact. He calls me his spiritual father, and I see myself 30 years ago in him. He not only has cameras that take stills and video, but sound equipment, and is going to be shooting the pilot for our multiplatform docuseries, *Suitcase on the Loose*.

Varial has flown over from Kota Kinabalu, the capital of Sabah. He went to Ulu Kalumpang Forest Reserve and filmed several pygmy elephants. There are only fifteen hundred to three thousand of these diminutive pachyderms in the world. Fourteen were poisoned in January 2013, and deforestation has claimed a huge amount of their habitat. Sabah lost nearly nine hundred thousand hectares of forest between 2001 and 2013, about 15 percent of its tree cover. Constricted habitat driven in large part by oil-palm expansion is squeezing elephants out of forests and into areas inhabited by humans, leading to increasing conflict and elephant slaughter. Sarawak's elephants and rhinos were wiped out long ago, and its only remaining orangutans are in the Semenggoh Wildlife Centre, near Kuching, and in Batang Ai National Park, three hundred miles southeast, on the Kalimantan border.

Varial has found rooms for us at a cozy hotel on the second floor above an arcade of shops and restaurants. The people in Miri, as in most of Sarawak's cities and larger towns, are mostly Malays, Chinese, Indians, indigenous Melanau, and a smaller percentage of Iban and Bidayuh who have migrated from their home villages for employment.

Miri is where most of the state's milled lumber and processed oil palm is shipped to markets abroad. China has overtaken Japan as the biggest market for the state's hardwoods. Samling, the biggest lumber and palm-oil conglomerate, has a huge office building here. Established in 1963 and headquartered in Kuching, it is the oldest and biggest player in upstream forestry and oil-palm plantation agriculture in Sarawak. While being, according to its website, "committed to implementing sustainable forest management practices," Samling has a log production of 2 to 3 million square meters annually and 1.4 million hectares of forest concessions in Malaysia and 1.6 million in Guyana, and now it is getting into property development.

The mountainous, jungle-smothered heart of Borneo remained unpenetrated, one of the last blank spots, *terrae incognitae*, on the map of the world, through World War II. By the end of the 1930s, missionaries had managed to contact only some of the indigenous peoples in the interior, and the head hunting some of them still practiced was fading with the spread of the Gospel. In 1944 the British parachuted seven secret operatives, led by an upper-class adventurer named Tom Harrisson, into the territory of the Kelabit, one of the highland tribes. Their mission was to organize native resistance against the Japanese. Harrisson revived the head hunting, and as growing numbers of Japanese soldiers were being snuck up on and picked off by poison darts fired from the jungle and having their heads cut off, they became reluctant to venture into the interior.

Harrisson's power went to his head and he began to display the heads of Japanese soldiers on poles around his compound and to become increasingly like the deranged Colonel Kurtz in *Apocalypse Now*. After the war Harrisson became the head of the Sarawak Museum and did some important archaeological and natural history research, but because the expat community couldn't stand him, it managed to get the local authorities not to renew his residence permit in 1966, and he died in Thailand a year later.

Jimmy Parang (not his real name), our fixer, who has set up our camp with the Penan and the rest of our three-week safari in Sarawak, comes by in his silver Mitsubishi 4x4 pickup. He's a down-to-earth, laid-back guy in his forties, a member of one of the twenty-seven indigenous groups in the mountainous interior who are known collectively as the Orang Ulu, the people of the headwaters. Jimmy grew up deep in the forest in the interior. His neighbors were Penan, and he speaks their language, as well as English, which very few Penan do. He learned it in Miri, working as a clerk for a shipping company, then for a foreign NGO that was developing a sustainable model for the logging that was laying waste to Sarawak's rain forest. After two years, it was clear to Jimmy that the NGO was accomplishing nothing in the field, so he quit to become an activist. He also organizes scientific and media expeditions to Penan country, like Bruce Parry's BBC show on tribal people, which had several segments on the Penan a couple of years before. Jimmy estimates that only sixty *orang asing*, "foreigners," in all have come to see the Penan and how they live (not counting the tourists who come to Long Iman, their big longhouse just downriver from Gunung Mulu National Park). He spends the rest of his time GPS mapping the hunting territories of Orang Ulu communities and posting signs that he hopes will deter the logging companies from coming in and taking their trees, until the customary right to their forest, where they have hunted from time immemorial, is established. This is the big fight now. To stoke his nervous energy, he chain-smokes menthol cigarettes: Era, the local brand. The local grassroots organization he's working with, the Non-Timber Forest Products Exchange Programme, is getting the Penan to plant sago palm, one of their staple foods, on degraded forest, whose big trees have been cut down and dragged through it by Caterpillar tractors to deter further logging of any of the big trees that come back.

We head out in the pickup to buy provisions. In the supermarket the cheapest vegetable oil has palm olein. So does Carnation evaporated milk, and the crackers, pasta, jar of peanut butter, and several dozen paper containers of freeze-dried noodle soup we throw into our cart. "A lot of stuff around the world says just vegetable oil," Jimmy says. "They don't identify that it's palm oil." (Norway contributes cans of "palm olein oil fortified with vitamin A" to the World Food Programme, which sends it to places like South Korea.) We add a fifty-pound bag of rice, coffee, tins of sardines, four sets of plates and glasses and cutlery, a big cook pot and a frying pan and spatula, a big rack of plastic-bottled water.

"We have to bring in our food because the nomadics don't have enough even for themselves," Jimmy whispers at the checkout counter. "If they ask why you need all this stuff, say we're going to Mulu National Park, not to the Penan. Foreign activists, outside agitators, are not popular in Sarawak." There was actually a price of $25,000 on the head of Bruno Manser, the Swiss champion of the Penan, who disappeared in the forest in 2000 and whose fate is still unknown; and Biruté Mary Galdikas told me she was held captive in Kalimantan for several days by some thugs hired by one of the big logging companies. They roughed her up but finally let her go with the warning that if she kept making trouble, next time they wouldn't go so easy on her.

As we load up the pickup in the hot midday sun, Christmas carols are incongruously being blasted from overhead speakers all over the city. We pick up a gas cook stove and a bottle of propane; a jerrican for the gas for the generator Jimmy's friend is renting us, which Varial wants so he can recharge his cameras and review his footage; umbrellas; three-dollar sneakers with soccer cleats—the local footgear for running around in the muddy rain forest; flashlights and batteries; and a big tarp, then head down to the market and get onions, carrots, cabbage, and some of the local fruits: durian, mangosteen, lychee, *mbangan, rambutan*. Davie finds out that the word for *thank you* is *terima kasih*, and at each stall where the women bag our purchases and give us change, Davie bows, saying the words politely. The Penan have no traditional word for *thank you*, for when food is shared it is not a favor, but an obligation (although they do not share everything). They do have a phrase, *jian kenin*, much like the Awá's *katú*, which means "kind-hearted," and that, under the influence of the dominant culture, is increasingly used to express gratitude.

They also don't have a word for *hello*—neither does Malay—although there is a conventional phrase when people meet, or say good-bye, and departures tend to be drawn out by friendly warnings to the ones about to travel. "The Penans live in a kind of timeless world," Ian Mackenzie explained in one of his telephone tutorials. "People who grow things keep track of time, but in the forest there is no need." Every day on the equator has twelve hours of daylight and twelve of night. The sun rises and sets at six with only a few minutes of variation. There are seasons of more or less rain, but in a rain forest there is never real drought (not until the trees are taken down; the Amazon has had two megadroughts in the last ten years, and Mexico's deforested Selva Maya is having a big *sequía* now). It's important to be aware of the rainfall cycles, because they govern what is in flower, and when a tree is in fruit, the animals come to eat it, and that means meat for the Penan. There is no word for *religion*. Nor for *homosexuality*. When it occurs, usually in the context of adolescent sexual experimentation, no one pays any attention; the concepts of homosexuality and lesbianism, so problematic in many cultures, simply do not exist. No word for *forest*, either. Not a lot of abstractions in Penan thinking. Galang's autobiography begins: "When I fell from my mother's belly, we Penans did not know about weeks, nor moons other than the moon in the sky, nor years other than the year of many fruits."

Into the Commodified Landscape

In the morning Jimmy picks us up. Our provisions and gear are in back, covered with the tarp and lashed down. We head out of Miri. "It will take at least eight hours to get to the Ba Marong (the band of Penan we are camping with), then we have to find where they are," Jimmy says. "I may have to track them with my headlights. Not every guide can do this." That should be interesting.

On the outskirts of the city we pick up a young woman named Christina, our first Penan. She has been visiting family. Jimmy is giving her a lift to her longhouse. She is wearing a Twitter T-shirt and sits in back between Varial and Davie, not saying a word the whole time except for a few chats in Penan on her cell phone. Like many of today's indigenous people, Christina cannot really be said to be traditional; Jared Diamond's *transitional* is a better word. Two years ago in Kalimantan, I went into the forest with some local Dayak teenagers who were working at one of Biruté Mary Galdikas's orangutan facilities. They were excellent tree climbers and could imitate the birds so well the birds answered them, but they also had cell phones and were Facebooking every chance they got. In another generation their tree-climbing and bird-imitating skills will probably be gone.

Varial found an earlier-stage transition in Bameno, one of the more acculturated villages of the Waorani people in the Ecuadorian Amazon, where he spent several weeks last year. They didn't have cell phones or Internet yet. The young chief had to travel forty kilometers to get online, which he was increasingly having to do. The people of the village still farmed and hunted and fished and the village was not far from the Intangible Zone, where there were still some hostile uncontacted bands they were cousins of. Yet they wore T-shirts, shorts, and flip-flops, no different from the general Ecuadorian population.

One morning, a helicopter arrived. "Quick," the Waorani of Bameno called to each other. "They're coming!" Off with the clothes and on with the feathers and body paint. Out stepped an immaculately coiffed safari-jacketed correspondent from NBC news, Ann Curry, who was greeted by a group from the village dancing naked for the cameras. They stayed for four hours, and Varial filmed the NBC crew filming the Waorani. After they left, the villagers put on their shorts and T-shirts again and split the pesos they got for the show. This is how it is in the modern tribal world. Varial is calling his film *Contacted*.

No one knows how many Penan there are. There are some in Kalimantan who are called Penan but Ian Mackenzie says they are a different people, and some in Brunei who are Eastern Penan, like the ones we are on our way to meet. They speak the same language. The Western Penan, who live closer to Kuching, are more acculturated and speak a different language, about as different as Spanish is from Portuguese, but they are still Penan. By some estimates, they number five thousand, and there may be as many as ten thousand Eastern Penan, who live in eighty-some communities, almost all named for the *long*, or mouth of the river that drains their territory. Except for several dozen Penan who are still seminomadic, they all live in modern longhouses, lines of connected one- or two-story apartments with a common roof, arcade, and balconies on the second story, if there is one. The Ba Marong are a young group, with lots of kids, Jimmy tells me. Only a few of them are over forty. They want to live traditionally, moving around in the forest, not in longhouses, but their forest is under assault. The logging company that cut the biggest trees twenty-five years ago wants to come in and do a second cut. The customary territory of each Penan group is called *tana'*, which is often mistranslated as "forest." *Tana'* means "land," which was assumed to be covered with trees, because that is all the Penan ever knew. But this is increasingly less the case now. The biggest trees have been removed from many of their *tana'*.

We pass Lambir Hills National Park, touted as having possibly the highest tree diversity of any forest in the Old World. Its tree species per hectare count is only slightly surpassed in Ecuador's Yasuní region. The park is 6,952 hectares (17,180 acres) and is one of the few remaining patches of undisturbed lowland Borneo rain forest in Sarawak.

For long periods, when much of the Earth's water was frozen in glaciers, Borneo was not an island—it has been an island, most recently, for only the last thirteen thousand years. During most of its history, Borneo's rain forest was connected to the Malaysian mainland. Both are part of the Southeast Asian rain forest, the oldest forest on Earth. There are relatively undisturbed tracts in Sarawak and on the mainland that date to 130 million years old, 70 million years older than the Amazon rain forest. Borneo's forest, as Dr. Galdikas's student Janie Dubman told me and later e-mailed a scientific paper about, is the most species-rich on Earth. It is thought to have fifteen thousand species of higher plants, ten thousand of which are endemic: they evolved in Borneo and are found nowhere else, like one species of the putrid-smelling vine parasite *Rafflesia*, whose flowers are the size of tires, named for Sir Thomas Stamford Raffles, the leader of the expedition that discovered the first member of the genus, in the Indonesian rain forest in 1818. But every time botanists go out, they find new species. The same is true of the entomologists. Twenty thousand insect species have been identified in Sarawak's Gunung Mulu National Park alone. Fantastic butterflies and moths, like the gigantic Rajah Brooke birdwing, have come into being in this ancient rain forest.

Borneo is a naturalist's paradise. It was here in 1856 that Alfred Russel Wallace (the Victorian naturalist and biogeographer for whom the

Wallace Line, which separates the ecozones of Asia and Wallacea, a transitional zone between Asia and Australia, is named), after examining the variation in some *Papilio*, or swallowtail, butterflies he had just collected, fell into a feverish, possibly malarial state and independently hit upon the theory of natural selection. Two years later he published a short paper, "On the Tendency of Varieties to Depart from the Original Type," which outlined the theory three years before Darwin was able to publish his massive substantiation of it, *The Origin of Species*, which he'd been working on for twenty years. Wallace always magnanimously referred to it as Darwin's theory.

Before coming to Borneo, he spent six years in the Amazon collecting bird and mammal skins and butterflies with Henry Walter Bates, another of the great Victorian naturalists. But on the way back to England with his specimens, which he was expecting to scrutinize minutely and live comfortably off the sale of for the rest of his days, the ship caught fire off Venezuela, and he lost everything. There is a moving passage about the pain of that loss at the end of his book *A Narrative of Travels on the Amazon and Rio Negro*. This necessitated a change of plans: eight life-changing years on Borneo, from which he returned a spiritualist, having been deeply affected by the ancestor worship of the local Dayak. In London, he held séances with the likes of Arthur Conan Doyle, Elizabeth Barrett Browning, and Francis Galton. For this, Wallace was criticized by Bates, Thomas Huxley, and Darwin, who found him "overly credulous" in his contention that consciousness is ultimately not physical in origin and that the dead are not really dead, and that it is possible to communicate with them.

Two hundred and fifty of Borneo's 380 dipterocarp species (out of the 500 in existence) are endemic, and one of them, *Shorea faguetana*, is the tallest tropical tree on Earth, reaching up to 290 feet. The ten most sought-after hardwoods by the logging companies are all dipterocarps. Every three to ten years, the El Niño cycle of the Southern Oscillation triggers a mass flowering. It's the greatest flower show on Earth. Eighty to 93 percent of the emergent dipterocarps blossom at once. One tree can produce four million flowers. The emergent (so called because, as the tallest of the trees, they emerge from the canopy) dipterocarps are not scattered individually, poking up here and there in the forest; they tend to grow in clusters, displaying patches of glorious color—snow white, yellow, blood orange, mauve—for an acre or two. But with most of the forest gone, or the big dipterocarps selectively logged, not many of such spectacular patches remain. The whole phenomenon is going the way of so many wonders of Borneo, and of the world.

We pass some Iban longhouses. Their forest is almost gone but they have satellite dishes for TV and Internet. Most of these Iban are working for the palm growers, Jimmy says. The Iban are the largest of the 40-some indigenous groups with distinct languages in Sarawak. They number about half a million. And they used to be called Sea Dayaks, pirates who came up from western Kalimantan starting in the fifteenth or sixteenth century and raided and subjugated and decapitated the people on the northwest coast, especially their chiefs. The skulls were hung as trophies in bundles over the hearths in their longhouses. By the nineteenth century northwestern Borneo was in a state of anarchy and the pirates were threatening to bring down the sultanate of Brunei, which had been going since the fourteenth century. In 1838 a remarkable thirty-five-year-old Englishman named James Brooke arrived in Sarawak, as the city of Kuching was called, in the *Royalist*, a 142-ton schooner he had purchased with an inheritance. Brooke had grown up in British India but had none of the typical colonial snobbishness against "the wogs" and was exploring the trading possibilities of the Malay Archipelago. The sultan's uncle enlisted him to crush the Sea Dayaks and a rebellion of a local people, the Bidayuh, which Brooke did, showing himself to be a talented military strategist and diplomat, who treated all sides fairly, and providing a new template for the governance of the unruly region. With peace restored and taxes flowing again to the sultan's coffers, the sultan in 1841 gratefully gave Brooke Sarawak, whose boundaries were dramatically extended during his reign and those of his nephew and his nephew's son, until by the end of their benign hundred-year dynasty, when it became a British colony, it had reached its present dimensions and is now the largest of Malaysia's thirteen states.

The Sea Dayak became the Iban and have adapted to the modern world—most of the government ministers in Kuching are Iban, even though Chief Minister Taib is Melanau, another tribe of northwestern

Borneo—but many, while nominally Christian, are said to retain their traditional religion, which has a supreme being called Bunsu Petara, and seven other deities.

These Iban are living now in what Peter Brosius, an anthropologist who studied the Western Penan in the 1990s, called "a commodified landscape." Ninety-five percent of the landscape here is a tossing sea of oil palm. Jimmy says that a ten-thousand-hectare oil-palm estate can generate a 26 percent annual profit. Most of the workers are brought in from Indonesia. They clear a dollar a day and come with their families and never leave the plantations. They have their own company store, clinic, and mosque. They work in pairs, cutting the fruit clusters on a hectare of trees per day. The industry is predicated on having this source of cheap labor. It is rife with child slavery and other human-rights problems.

For the rest of the day we drive through nothing but oil-palm trees planted on scalped little hills that used to be smothered with rain forest, the younger trees a sheaf of pinnate fronds, the older ones with plated trunks and the fronds shooting out from their crowns like monstrous carrot tops. Liberia has just leased a million hectares to Sime Darby and Boustead, the London company that introduced the plant to Malaya in 1910 and put in the first plantations. The palm oil will be shipped to Europe and used for biofuel. The perversity of this is quite staggering: obliterate the rain forest and pour gigatons of carbon into the atmosphere from its incineration so internal-combustion engines up north can have a "clean" green fuel to run on? Sacrifice Africa so Europe can feel less guilty about its emissions? And now Uganda has approved massive palm planting on the Ssese Islands in Lake Victoria, which have some of the highest levels of endemic biodiversity anywhere.

The tragedy of Sarawak is that half of its forest, including 90 percent of its lowland Borneo rain forest, has been logged at least once, and much of it converted to palm oil plantations, but palm oil is only the fourth-largest source of revenue for Malaysia. And to put the $40 billion industry into perspective globally, crimes affecting natural resources and the environment inflict damage on developing countries amounting to more than $70 billion, according to the Wildlife Conservation Society. Wildlife trafficking, the illegal trade in elephant ivory, rhino horn, tiger skins, bear gall bladder, and other animal parts, is estimated to be worth $17 billion. The rest is trafficking in timber, mainly tropical hardwoods. The timber is worth more than the palm oil, but is a one-shot deal, while palm oil is long-term "sustainable" revenue. Varial sets up a GoPro camera on the hood of the truck, which captures millions of palms bristling with health on the foothills of the mountains, whose blue ridgelines we are beginning to catch glimpses of in the distance.

The road we're driving on, built by the Chinese, is new and, for the time being, smooth. Soon it will be cracked and full of potholes, like the roads the Chinese have been building all over Africa. "Nothing made by the Chinese lasts," Jimmy observes. The architecture of the few buildings we pass is generic tropical moderne, nothing to suggest we are on Borneo any more than Mexico or Brazil. But Sarawak is clearly more developed, visibly better off than Kalimantan. "Malaysia is richer than Indonesia," Jimmy tells us. "The distribution of wealth is thirty-five thousand *ringgit* [eleven thousand dollars] per capita, three times more than Indonesia's, but if you go to villages, ask what they earn. The per capita might be zero because they just depend on the forest and subsistence farming."

Every once in a while we pass a compound for Chinese employees of the logging or palm-oil companies, or a Chinese-built hospital, or a kitschy Chinese Buddhist cemetery. "People are dying to get in there," Jimmy quips. The Chinese population here, at least the managerial class, is large and growing, as it is in Africa. Jimmy has a droll sense of humor. He is amused by his Western *orang asing* clients' "green hell" and "emerald forest" fantasies about Borneo. Some are expecting to meet noble savages, others are expecting poisonous snakes draped on every branch. We will be encountering the reality soon enough.

We reach the Baram River at a trading center called Long Lama just at that magic moment in the tropics, fifteen minutes before sunset, when the foliage becomes iridescent blue and everything glows softly for a minute or so. The phenomenon, as I understand it, is caused by the horizontal shafts of the sinking sun being filtered through surface vapor, which produces a sudden change in color temperature like alpenglow, except objects are illuminated by the cool instead of the hot end of the spectrum. I watch the leaves of a tree on the riverbank undergo this evanescent, incandescent transformation. The tree is scored with ancient vees—a rubber tree. The white latex that oozed down the vees was collected in cups. A remnant of Malaysia's last big monoculture, started by seeds smuggled or legally exported from the Amazon by Henry Wickham in 1876, the new Malaysian plantations put an end to the Amazon's rubber boom, but their profitability ended by the time the country became independent. Malaysia is still one the world's biggest natural latex producers, along with Indonesia and Thailand, but most of the global demand is supplied by synthetic rubber now. Something else had to fuel the new country's economy, and that new commodity, disastrous for its biological and cultural diversity, was palm oil.

Jimmy explains that six dams are planned for the Baram, while on the Batang Rajang River, a hundred miles south, the Murum Dam is finished but the water has not been impounded because Bakun Dam, fifty miles west of Murum, which is up and running, displaced fifteen hundred Western Penan who still haven't been resettled. There is a lawsuit to stop the same thing from happening at Bakun, while four more dams are to be built by 2020 by the Chinese company that built the Three Gorges Dam.

Jimmy drives the pickup onto the ferry. On the other side of the river the paved highway soon ends and the land of the Orang Ulu begins; the converted zone, the commodified landscape, gives way to the tribal zone, the real Borneo we have come to see. But in fact we can't see because it is dark now—I won't realize it till we return three weeks later on the same road—but there is still nothing but oil palm for several hours.

The first people to settle on Borneo, forty thousand years ago, whose remains were found by Tom Harrisson in the Great Cave of Niah, were part of the original migration out of Africa. They were, according to Ian Mackenzie, dark skinned, with kinky hair, like the indigenous people of Papua New Guinea, Australia, and Melanesia. Another wave of people, lighter-skinned Asiatic people with the epicanthic fold on their upper eyelids, came down in boats from islands like Taiwan ten to four thousand years ago, when the Pleistocene glaciation had melted. The sea had risen and there was no longer a land bridge to the mainland. Borneo was now an island, part of the Malay Archipelago. These new humans had been farmers, and found a land of unimaginable plenty with little competition. Some of these people settled along the central spine of the island that runs down from Sabah—where the biggest mountain, Kinabalu (13,435 feet), rises—in a southwesterly arc that divides Malaysian Borneo and Brunei from Kalimantan. Kinabalu is the world's most recent pluton, an extrusion of molten granodiorites that burst through the layers of sediment on the edge of the Sunda tectonic plate ten million years ago, after they had been heaved up into the central ridge by the Australian tectonic plate ramming into it. The ridge runs south then southwest toward Kuching. Ridges and innumerable subridges and buttressing ribs thereof, divided by deep mist-shrouded valleys with torrential streams, break off either side of the main spine. Here and there needles of razor-sharp white pinnacle karst, of ancient marine origin, thrust up from the forest canopy.

The people who settled in the mountainous interior became known as the Orang Ulu, the people of the headwaters, because on the north side of the central ridge they were in the Middle and Upper Baram river valley. They belong to some twenty-seven groups, including Bukitan, Bisaya, Kayan, Kajang, Kelabit, Kenyah, Lugat, Lisum, Murut, Penan, Sian, Tabun, Ukit, and Saban. Eastern and Western Penan speak different but linguistically related languages—while Murut, Lun Bawang, and Kelabit all speak the same language. *Orang* means "people." *Orang asing* are people from outside, foreigners. *Orang utan* means "person of the forest." This was popularized by the Dutch into the meaning *orangutan* has today.

The Penan and about a score of other highland ethnic groups remained nomadic hunter-gatherers into historic times. The other Orang Ulu lived in settled communities, in longhouses, and farmed and supplemented what they grew with game, fruits, nuts, and other plant food from the forest. Domesticated pigs and fish caught in the rivers were their main source of protein, and still are. But the Penan saw that the food in the forest was so abundant that they didn't need to farm at all. There were half a dozen different species of palm in the forest, the most important of which was sago (*Eugeissona utilis*), that provided them with all the carbohydrates they needed, and huge herds of wild pigs, or *babui*, and many kinds of monkeys and deer for protein, so they gravitated to the nomadic hunter-gatherer lifestyle. This lifestyle was not a cultural devolution, but adaptation to new ecological circumstances. Now they were living in a kind of paradise, in midelevation rain forest at about two or three thousand feet or more, right on the equator. So the temperature was always perfect in this land of ridges and deep valleys filled with white mist and clear, strong rivers. Every day was a new adventure as they went out into it to see what the pickings were. It was always full of surprises, marvelous new things to learn about, a birdsong they had never heard before, a waterfall none of them had ever bathed in. The forest was all they knew. It was their universe. Learning how to survive in it and to live respectfully in it, without disturbing the living or the dead, whose ghosts were wandering around in it, or the spirits of the animals and the trees, was a completely absorbing, lifelong process.

Day after day, year after year, the sun rose and set at six. Another day in paradise. The Penan are no good at dates. The old people who have a sense of the past speak of *rajahs*, "reigns" or "political regimes." Rajah Brooke, the three generations of enlightened white Rajahs of Sarawak—James (on whom Joseph Conrad's *Lord Jim* is based), his nephew John Johnson-Brooke and John's son Charles—lasted from 1841 to the Second World War. It is remembered as a golden age in which the Penan and their forest were left alone. The Brookes respected the Orang Ulu and their right to live the way they were living. They treated everybody fairly, and everybody in Sarawak looked up to them because the peace and order they brought and presided over were unprecedented. Then came Rajah Japan, a time of occupation and brutal atrocities that lasted only a few years. Then Rajah George and Rajah Elizabeth, when Borneo was part of British Malaya, then, in 1962, Rajah Independence, which has not been good to the Orang Ulu. It brought the chain saw and the Caterpillar tractor, as Kuala Lumpur went on a binge of oil-palm growing. There is no place left in Sarawak where the emergent dipterocarps can't be gotten to and harvested. For the last quarter-century, they have endured Rajah Taib, the end of the

Penan and their forest. The apocalypse, unless something can be done about it.

Overnight in Long Karanan

It starts to rain torrentially. The wet season is beginning. Progress on the steep logging roads becomes slow and treacherously slippery. Only Jimmy's furious last-minute steering barely keeps us from plunging off into a deep gorge. We pass trucks laden with huge logs, pulled over because the conditions are too dangerous, and others barreling toward us. Finally at about nine we reach Christina's longhouse, Long Karanan (that's what the road sign says, but it's usually spelled *Kerangan*), where we decide to spend the night. The longhouse is divided into a dozen flats, each inhabited by an extended family. Its zinc shed roof extends over a common fenced concrete walkway. A small shop on one end sells junk food, cigarettes, and soda. Inside Christina's family's flat is a large room floored with linoleum. Several kids and women are watching a television mounted on one of the walls—some soap opera from Singapore, whose young stars periodically burst into pop love songs. Further in are two small bedrooms and the kitchen. Beans are boiling on a gas stove. A woman is washing vegetables in the sink. In back are several large barrels of water with a faucet for doing laundry, and the outhouse.

"The Penan here were living in huts in the forest and slowly built this longhouse, learning little by little," Jimmy tells us. "Maybe they did ninety percent of the work. They had to buy chain saws. The government provided a water purifier, which is useless because they cook their water. But one of chief minister's cronies sells the water purifier. The laptop and small notebooks are sold to schools for five thousand to six thousand ringgit by the company of another crony. If you go to a computer store you can easily get one for eight hundred. These communities are always on the short end of the stick because the government gives their land to Taib's cronies. Of course they contribute royalties and taxes. And every time the government gives land the chief minister gets a cut. The only way to stop this is to change the government. Harrison Ngau, a lawyer who has been fighting Taib and filing indigenous land claims with the courts for years, is the opposition party candidate for chief minister, but his party has to win at least half of the seventy-one seats in the parliament for him to get the job. Taib's party has forty-five seats, and the opposition party, actually a coalition of opposition parties, has only seven."

After day breaks I go down to the river, which curves sharply around a wall of shale below the longhouse, and ease into the muddy brown water. A young woman comes down after a few minutes and, giggling, performs her ablutions facing the other way. Across the river is thick rain forest. A bird calls out in measured four-note bars, sounding like a bell chime, or a cell phone ring. Back at the longhouse the other families act as if our presence is nothing out of the ordinary and respect our space. Many of the apartments are empty, which is usually the case with these new Penan longhouses. The old anarchy and freedom of movement is still in effect. People come and go as they please. Some are in the forest hunting and collecting food. Some are in Long Bedian, the Kayan trading center for the Middle Baram area. Others are making money in various ways, however they can, including working for the loggers and palm growers.

In the large clearing in front of the longhouse a juvenile *babui*, a wild pig (Bornean bearded pig, *Sus barbatus*) is chasing a boy on a dirt bike. It is an *olong*, Jimmy tells us. An *olong* is a pet, the orphan of game the men shot they bring in to be adopted as a member of the family until it is old enough to go back to the forest and make it on its own. Most *olong* are pigs or monkeys. It is taboo to kill and eat an *olong*, although in special cases, after a meeting of the community and the consent of the head man, it does happen. The Awá of Amazonia I was just with in June do the same thing, to the point that the women suckle monkeys orphaned by their husbands as if they were their own babies.

Molong, the verb of *olong*, has several other meanings. If you *molong* a sago palm, you lay claim to it for your family's exclusive use; no one else can harvest it because you are going to. *Molong* also means not taking any more than you need, but Mackenzie says this meaning is a romantic projection of Westerners, specifically Peter Brosius, the anthropologist who studied the Western Penan in the late 1980s. Ian insists the meaning does not exist in Eastern Penan; nonetheless, we soon will find *molong* being used in this way in our encampment with the Ba Marong, and in two other Penan communities we will visit, so it seems to be in circulation, and is probably a recent borrow—from the Western perception that they have this concept. An example of how the observer can impact the observed.

This obviously has an appeal to modern activists trying to stop or at least reduce the destruction of the planet's biocultural diversity, knowing that the last hunter-gatherers—who we were, originally—don't take any more than they need, they live lightly on the land, have a minimal footprint, in current parlance. If the Penan don't have it explicitly, it is a concept with similar iterations in many indigenous subsistence cultures that modern industrial society seems to have pretty much thrown out the window and might do well to revisit. Obviously if the forest is going to provide you with what you need, you can't clean it out. But with the need for cash and a market for bushmeat in Long Bedian, and more Penan hunting with shotguns, the game is getting scarce—as with the Awá, and the Mekranoti I visited in 1975, who had been contacted only fourteen years before but had shotguns and were already having to go hours further out from their village to find meat than when they hunted with bows and arrows.

The notion of the "ecologically noble savage," that all indigenous people are great conservationists and have deep reverence for other living things, was debunked by the conservation biologist Kent Redford in 1990, who provided numerous examples of gratuitous slaughter of the animals they depend or depended on at the time. I myself have had some disillusioning experiences. In 1975, I was traveling through the forest with a young Waika Yanomami who ripped off the plastron of a *jaboti* tortoise he had just caught and poked its still-beating heart and penis, gratuitously torturing it before tossing it, still alive, to roast on the fire. In 1984, ascending the Nhamundá River, in the lower Amazon, I passed a charred black ten-mile stretch on the right bank that the young Indian with me admitted to having torched "for the fun of it." But the damage indigenous people have done to their ecosystems and their fellow beings took place in the context of an abundance that no longer exists, and is nothing compared to profit-motivated modern industrial operations with chain saws and bulldozers. The Penan don't have the equipment or the numbers or the interest in destroying the forest. Why would they kill more animals than they need to—they would have to carry the meat around, and it would soon rot—unless they are taking it to sell in Long Bedian? So this meaning of *molong*, the notion that the Penan are in equilibrium with and part of their ecosystem, is not entirely a romantic projection.

The Eastern Penan we will be with seem to genuinely believe in this Western meaning of *molong* now, they have incorporated it, the same way they have superimposed the Judeo-Christian supreme God onto their much more complicated pantheon of spirits, and to some extent they have always believed in it, although Mackenzie says if the Penan see a deer in the forest, they're not going to say, it's pregnant, or, we have been eating a lot of deer lately, so let's give this one a pass. In any case, *molong* is an important concept for the marketing of their brand, one of the main things the Penan have to offer the modern world, which is what has to be done now if they are going to retain a semblance of their culture. But also, it seems an example of how the preconceptions and the cultural and cognitive frameworks of even the most conscientiously "impartial" outside observer can shape his perception of what he is trying to understand. The fifth edition of the *American Heritage Dictionary* cites my usage of *projection* in the meaning denoting the attribution of one's own attitudes, feelings, or suppositions to others: "Even trained anthropologists have been guilty of unconscious projection—of clothing the subjects of their research in theories brought with them into the field."

A gecko is chucking and clicking on the railing of the porch where Davie and I are sitting, watching the *molong babui* running behind the teenager on the dirt bike, having the time of his life, following him everywhere like puppy. I photograph a tailless (as opposed to the swallowtails in Bedford) black *Papilio* drinking nectar from the red flowers of a bush in front of the porch with a blurred flurry of its wings. Nine hundred fifty-six species of Papilionidae, 10 percent of which are endemic, have been collected on the island, including the spectacular Rajah Brooke birdwing, named by Wallace for James Brooke, who gave him full support when he arrived in Kuching in 1856; and ones from which Wallace formulated his own theory of evolution two years later. According to the World Wildlife Fund, eleven thousand species of Lepidoptera—butterflies and moths—have been found on Borneo. Ten percent are endemic, 75 percent are found only in the Sunda Shelf archipelagic bioregion (which Wallace distinguished from the Indochinese bioregion in his biogeography of the Malay Archipelago). No one knows how many more there are.

This is only the second rain forest Davie has ever been in—a couple of years ago he went to an *ayahuasca* camp in Ecuador—and he is loving it, feeling completely at home and engaged in these woods. We keep remembering random things about our childhood, like how we used to steal cigarettes from our parents' silver boxes, which we used to take around to the guests at their cocktail parties, and smoke them in the Phillips' woods. Davie remembers our secret code for this—purpling bubblegum—and how one time I said to him in the kitchen where his mom was cooking dinner, "Hey Davie, howsabout we go purple some bubblegum?" and she figured it out immediately and we were busted big time. Davie recalls that he also bought cigs from a machine in The Carousel, an Italian restaurant in the village. In those days you didn't have to be eighteen.

"The first time I went there," he says, "I was like thirteen and I asked the guy at the cash register how much they were, and he said, in a thick Italian accent, what I thought was 'certified'—but I gradually realized was 'thirty-five'—cents." I tell him my brother once saw Frank Costello, the Mafia don, step out of a limo and go into The Carousel for lunch. The madeleines of our boyhood just keep coming, and as we savor newly retrieved memories of half a century ago, we are at the same time soaking up the amazing pageant of life in the upper reaches of the cut-over but still riotous Borneo lowland rain forest. Davie, as I knew he would be, is proving to be the perfect traveling companion, never complaining, never asking for help in spite of his handicap, always thinking of others and how he can be helpful, no ego to clash with, which can ruin a trip like this.

Back in the pickup, we rise into a dramatic highlands of knife-edge ridges dissected by deep valleys with mist licking their floors and their sheer walls coated with what is still, up to three thousand feet, Bornean lowland rain forest. To the right a six-hundred-foot jungle-smothered spire of white pinnacle karst looms. To its immediate right a long, thin waterfall is spilling over a ledge. My great-uncle Avinoff would have made a painting of it, like the "dreamland of tropical splendor" series he did of the mountainous interior of Jamaica.

One of the ridgetops affords a vista of fifty miles of nothing but rain forest, a spectacular world-class wilderness. With the Mulu massif rising in the distance, and mist swirling the valleys, it's like the Creator outdid himself, an epic, distinctive landscape, like Yosemite, once seen, never forgotten. We can see so far the curvature of the Earth is apparent. But on closer inspection all the ridges in the foreground have logging roads on them, like the ones we are on, and eroded gashes where the big commercial dipterocarps, *meranti*, *kapur*, *kerning*, *nyatoh*, *zupater*, and half a dozen other species, were limbed and cut into thirty- to forty-foot lengths and slid down to the valley floors, where we can hear the rumble of logging trucks. So it's more like a scarred Garden of Eden, paradise violated, a *desecration*, in Wendell Berry's term, stripped of the emergents except for the *gita* (*Alstonia pneumatophora*) trees, whose slender white candelabras shoot up two hundred feet, way above the canopy. Their wood is too soft to be of commercial interest and is used to make the *sape* (pronounced sa-PAY), the traditional sitar-like stringed instrument of the Orang Ulu. We're going to visit one of the Penans' master *sape* players after camping with the Ba Marong.

Jimmy has been GPS mapping the Penans' customary territories so they can be recognized by the court in Kuching, the state capital, and protected from the logging, oil-palm, and hydro-dam companies. He is under no illusion how hard a battle this is, because the boards of these companies are full of state ministers and relatives and cronies of Taib. "The logging companies come back four or five times," he explains. "It never ends unless the license is nullified by proof that the concession is in customary indigenous territory. I have GPS mapped Ba Marong, but I have to get Kenyah and Kayan hunting territory recognized as precedent. The law says you have to have been using the land since 1956 for it to be customary, but it only applies to land being farmed, not forest that is being hunted. We have a lot of cases that we won in court, but the government never respected the decision of its own judges. Right now there are more than two hundred cases in court for the native people. The problem with the Penan is that some of them are being paid monthly stipends by the logging companies, so they're against keeping them out and are letting them cut what they want, and they're being used to persuade the holdouts. All we can do is keep filing customary claims until there are enough of them, along with peaceful protests and international pressure, that they are respected."

In 2010 British investigative journalist Clare Rewcastle-Brown founded *Sarawak Report* and its sister organization Radio Free Sarawak to expose the massive corruption in the selling out of the state's rain forest, indigenous people, and biodiversity. She recently flew into Kuching but they wouldn't let her out of the airport. Sophie Grig, the director Survival International's Borneo campaign, sent me a new report about how Penan girls who get lifts to school from logging truckers are sometimes raped, and they have no recourse. The police couldn't care less.

In September 2013 the actor Harrison Ford, one of the hosts and reporters for a Showtime docuseries on the human hand in climate change, *Years of Living Dangerously*, was threatened with expulsion after a confrontational interview with Indonesia's minister of forestry about the devastating assault on its rain forests by the logging and palm-oil companies that it is doing nothing about and is in fact facilitating. But these exposés and harangues by foreigners are having little effect in the countries themselves or on their governments. Maybe a concerted all-court press, including leveraging companies that buy palm oil and rallying individual consumers to boycott it, will eventually cause a wave to crest in the zeitgeist, as is being done with ivory and fossil fuel. "We have to keep the pressure on," Jimmy says.

An old man and his wife have walked up from a modern longhouse below the road and are waiting for us. The man is named Rajah Jamale. He used to be the headman of Ba Marong. Mackenzie explains there are no chiefs in Penan society. Like most hunter-gatherers, they are very egalitarian. Everybody comes and goes and does what he pleases. There are headmen, usually more than one elder in the community who are recognized as having the moral authority to lead their people. The position is informal and not permanent, but often hereditary, because the traits are often passed from father to son. Rajah's father was headman of Ba Marong before him, and his son is now. Rajah is in his late fifties and has black hair in a bowl-shaped haircut, holes the size of quarters in his ears, and a beautiful blue-and-white-bead necklace, strung by his wife, Akons. The Penan are famous for their bead- and basketwork. Rajah is carrying a short blowgun, three feet long, with a spearhead on the end, and a bamboo cylinder containing poison darts is strapped around his waist. He is smartly dressed in a blue baseball cap, soccer shorts, and T-shirt, and the white sneakers with the rubber spikes that we bought for ourselves in Miri. Akons, we will discover, plays a mean jaw harp. The Penan lamellophone is a delicate piece of craftsmanship, with the tongue and frame carved from the same piece of wood. They are a handsome couple, genuine, caring, clean souled, grounded, the sort of people Penan describe with the interchangeable terms *jian adet* or *jian barék*, good people who follow the norms. Like people I know back home, the bulwark of every society. The two of them climb in back.

The road goes down into valleys, over bridges, forks into several roads, each going up a separate ridge. Each ridge we ascend is higher, until we are close to 2,500 feet. We pass a sign saying that the Samling Group of Companies has the license to log here. All the big trees were taken out twenty-five years ago. Now they're coming back for the second cut, Jimmy explains. A few miles of dips and rises on the ridge later, just after a stream coming down from its highest point, rising steeply and thickly forested to the left, we come to a place where laundry, including a bra, is hanging on a line between two poles and draped on bushes, and four dirt bikes are parked. We have arrived.

In Camp

The camp is 150 yards up a steep muddy path from the road. We can hear its human hum, chatter and laughter up in the trees. Several teenage boys come down and help us carry our gear and the boxes of food, and we follow them as they effortlessly negotiate vines, roots, brush, mud, and fallen trees up a newly hacked trail in flip-flops and bare feet, while we struggle and slip in our soccer-cleated sneakers. The trail goes up to a flat shelf with one gap in the trees that looks east, to the morning sun halfway up in the sky, and the next forested ridge and a maze of other ridges and mist-licked valleys going back behind it as far as you can see. On the shelf are four *jamin*, huts raised on four-foot poles lashed with rattan palm vines from the forest, with pole-slat floors. Traditionally, the roofs are thatched with palm fronds—three species are used—but these roofs are orange tarps. At the front of each hut's slatted-pole floor a fire is burning in an earthen hearth known as an *aveu*, metal pots hang over the flames, a stack of machete-split wood sits to one side. The interior of the hut is for sitting and eating, talking and sleeping, and weaving rattan.

Twenty-three of the thirty-five-member community are here. There are a lot of children. Everybody is under forty except for a stout, strong-faced woman in her fifties named Choeling, who is sitting in her hut, weaving nine-yard strands of rattan that cascade down its side. Her husband, the headman after Rajah, died last year. Rajah's son Sagung, the current headman, is married to her daughter. They are here with their five daughters. Christina, the twelve-year-old, is blossoming into a tall, slender beauty. These people are really good looking, glowing with health and well-being. Sagung has wispy mustaches, elaborate dragon tattoos on his arms and torso that he got from a Bidayuh (another tribe) master up on the main ridge, dozens of bracelets woven in several styles from various kinds of rattan, plastic rings, and a wristwatch for a touch of modern chic. He looks like Genghis Khan or a martial arts master. You could put him right in the movies.

In the other two huts are a young couple and their infant child, and three young women with their babies, as well as three teenage boys who migrate between the four huts. In fact everybody is constantly visiting each other's huts. It's a cozy scene, the way we should all be living, the way humans have lived from time immemorial, apart from a radio and CD player, flashlights, flip-flops and modern clothes, and other useful items from the world that is encroaching relentlessly. The kids are full of beans and constantly playing in the huts, in the forest, down by the stream. Davie has never seen kids get along so well. In ten days we won't see a single fight. Half a dozen emaciated dogs—Australian dingoes—are snoozing under the huts. The dogs go out with the hunters and come to life whenever something is being cooked and scraps and bones could be thrown their way. After the fourth day two almost full-grown *olong babui*, "wild pigs" orphaned by the hunters and adopted by the women and children, appear. They have tracked the band from their last camp, a couple of miles down in the valley below. They are starting to return to the forest, and after a day out exploring it, they came back to the camp and everybody was gone. They will become a noisy, nosy part of our ecosystem, sniffing and rooting everywhere at all hours, tearing up the used plastic diapers that the young women with babies throw under their hut, trying to raid the kitchen at night, raising the hackles of the dogs, who keep chasing them out only to have them return.

This camp is only three days old. The Ba Marong built it nearer the road than they usually do so it would be easier for us. And now they are camping within earshot of passing trucks, so they can monitor who is coming and going. A logging company that Jimmy says is called Melfra Keng claims it has a government license to cut in Ba Marong and wants to start. Sagung has told them over my dead body and that the Ba Marong will set up a blockade if necessary, by forming a human wall on the road along the ridge at the entrance to their *tana*', so Melfra Keng's logging trucks and Caterpillars can't get in. This is the only peaceful recourse the Orang Ulu have to stop the chain saws and dams. They started doing them in the 1980s, around the same time the rubber tappers in the Brazilian state of Acre independently and convergently started having their blockades, or *empates*, to stop the ranchers from cutting down their rain forest.

Jimmy is leaving us in the hands of Nelson, a Penan from a more assimilated community, Long Kerong, who speaks English, having worked for twelve years as a tourist guide at Mulu National Park, whose eastern border is several hours away. We have a cook, a young man also from Long Kerong who is eager to learn English so he can become an architect, if he can ever put together the money for the tuition, and in short order the two of them throw up a kitchen and a bench from saplings and rattan in the nearby forest and cover them with our tarp. Rajah and Akons build their own hut in the same style as the others. Davie says, "These huts are like the forts we used to build in the woods, only more sturdy."

We could move in with the Ba Marong in their huts, but decide to go with our Hennessy hammocks, stringing them and the tarps over them to the eight-to-ten-inch-thick dipterocarps that the camp is pitched in a grove of. The hammocks weigh nothing and are like

being in a little rain- and bug-proof cocoon that you get in and out of
through a Velcro-sealed slit at your feet. And I have a lightweight tropical sleeping bag that's no bigger and heavier. The rains started a week
ago, coming in the afternoon, and in torrential downpours through the
night. Mushrooms will be out in a month.

The tots have runny noses and are running low temperatures on and off,
and their mothers ask if we have medicine, which I do, a well-stocked
medicine cabinet this time because I am responsible for two others
besides me. We are covered for everything except snakebite. As in
many parts of the "developing" world, all white people are assumed
to be doctors. I give a mother one of the small aspirins I take daily
as a heart-attack preventative, and it seems to do some good for her
two-year-old daughter. But these balmy highlands are incredibly sa-
lubrious. I will lose twenty pounds on this three-week safari, and get
under two hundred for the first time in thirty years from a combination
of exercise and not eating processed food. There are few mosquitoes,
and no malaria up here. We are not taking Malarone, but have it with
us in case one of us comes down with the insect-borne disease, which
I have had twice and have no desire to be smitten with a third time.

I was worried about the leeches, but there are not many. Davie finds
an engorged one between his toes. But they are small and easily pinched
off, and their wound is antiseptic. These ones are like inchworms—
inch-and-a-half worms, more accurately—but you can feel the suction
on both ends as they move across your palm. Consider the leech, I think
as I pick one off my arm. One end is female, the other male. Leeches
are hermaphroditic. They lie in wait on leaves for a meal to pass by,
make a Y-shaped wound with their many-toothed jaws and inject an
anticoagulant into it to keep the blood flowing, and ingest several times
their weight in one meal. Opportunities to feed and mate are few and
far between, so they make the most of it, I guess. What purpose could
such vampiric, opportunistic creatures serve in the scheme of things,
apart from being food themselves for whoever eats them? Why do they
exist? I ask Sagung, and he says, "This is from the dead people who
become leeches and need to have blood." And I ask, "Taib, the chief
minister who is sucking the blood out of Sarawak, will he become a
leech?" This gets a laugh.

"This leech is called *kematek*," Sagung tells me. "We also have tiger leech, green and brown striped; it's longer. Also some in rivers."

"What about the purple millipede I found on the path up to our camp?" I ask. It was four inches long and when I approached curled up into a perfect question mark, as if it was asking, what is happening to my forest? "Why does the millipede have so many legs?" I ask Sagung, and he says, "Stay away from the *sagusap*. This millipede is part of the cobra's body. Long ago someone cut off part of the cobra—I don't know if it was the head or the tail—and by the end of the day it was getting rotten and started to grow legs and became a *sagusap*. If a millipede bites, you have to have as many doses of medicine as its legs. It's as poisonous as cobra."

We have no agenda here except to get to know these people. I am taking notes all the time, and Varial is taking pictures, and Davie is making himself useful, splitting firewood with one of their *parangs*, or "machetes," and handing it up to the women in the huts. Davie has gotten really good with his one arm in the last fifteen years. He is just really nice and so are they, and they like him because he is humble and always thinking about others and not being in anybody's way. On a basic human level, the Ba Marong are totally open and accessible and are eager to show us how happy they are in the forest and how much they love it. Having hung out with Amazon Indians, Pygmies (some of the most intelligent people I have ever met), and Bushmen, I know that their intellectual capacity and emotional range are no different from people in the modern world. The reason they are still hunter-gatherers is that their minds and beings are fully engaged in their unfathomably complex rain forest world, even though they have no word for *forest* or *world*.

The Mekranoti Kayapo, with whom I had spent a month in 1975, making the first collection of their medical plants, could recognize fifteen species of bee on the wing, and had names for each, but it took them forever to count to ten. They nicknamed me *No Ket*, "No Eyes," so oblivious was I of what was going on in the forest. Here, too, I am far from even getting to first base on the flora and fauna. Rajah thinks the birdcall I heard at Long Karanan is "son of hornbill. Adults do *Anh anh, Anh anh anh anh anh anh.*" Choeling says it's a mantis, but I'm sure it was a bird. I ask her if she knows that women mantises eat the men after copulation, and Choeling says, "Only they are allowed to." A bird lets out a series of rising then falling *skreeks*. Choeling says *puriwai*. Asian paradise flycatcher.

I ask Nelson one evening about the old religion, the nature-based animism, the multitiered cosmology that Ian Mackenzie has been telling me about. This is a touchy subject, particularly for a devout Christian like Nelson. Many elements of the old religion still persist but are often kept hidden, and much of it has been lost. Only a few of the old men, like Galang, Mackenzie's informant, are still in contact with the other worlds, or know the several thousand trees and their spirits, whose names, along with many of the *suket*, the myths of the Penan canon, will be gone in our lifetime, which is why Mackenzie's work is so important. Some Penan are embarrassed about their old beliefs, which the missionaries made them feel were pagan and backward, and don't like to talk about them, even though they are still afraid of the ghosts in the woods. The missionary whose Bible camp Galang attended—volume 1 of his memoirs devotes more than ten thousand words to her—was an Australian woman named Phyllis Webster, but the Penan called her Rungu. According to Mackenzie, she "targeted certain beliefs, those in competition with Christianity, such as about an afterlife, and about the healing powers of their shamans. But she didn't touch their belief in ghosts and evil spirits, because being an evangelical fundamentalist, she believed in them herself. Instead, she recast them as malevolent demons, 'satans', which you have to pray to the Lord Jesus to protect yourself against, like the two thousand unclean spirits He turned into pigs and drove off a cliff into the sea."

I recall the old Dayak in Kalimantan who was selling Biruté Mary Galdikas his forest because he was afraid the loggers would disturb the *gaip*, the little people who live in the deepest, darkest part of the forest, that they would become angry and give horrible diseases to him and his family if he let the loggers cut down their home. When I asked him (with Biruté translating) what spirits live in this forest, she said, "He doesn't believe in spirits except *sanyangwata*, who is the same as Jesus. He says there are no spirits here, none, but lots of snakes. He doesn't want to talk about it because you'll think he is uneducated. He's afraid of even mentioning the *gaip*, the little invisible people, lest they come after him for revealing their existence. He has a deep, not spiritual but practical connection to them. They are the forest elves you don't want to get on the wrong side of."

Galdikas writes in her memoir, *Reflections of Eden*, how she arrived in Borneo seduced by the sixties' romantic fallacy that "nature is pure and noble, beautiful and bright" and "produces happy endings," and soon found that the local Dayaks had a very different view of nature, that it was full of evil spirits, death, and deception, and that this world was not the real world, but a dream. She married a Dayak whose totem was a type of bamboo. "My husband refused to talk about his religion until I went into the interior and learned about it from an anthropologist who was living with some of its high priests," she told me. "The Dayaks believe we have two souls, darkness and light, life and death, male and female, good and evil, everything in the universe is divided in two. The ones who are ashamed of their beliefs convert to Islam, but never completely lose them. When you have those connections, you are not afraid of death because you go back to where you came from, to the real world; you wake up from this dream."

The richly varied animistic systems of the Dayak in Kalimantan are lumped together under the general term *Hindu Kaharingan*, not that they have anything to do with Hinduism, but because in Indonesia everybody has to have a religion, and since animism is not conceded to be one, and the indigenous people are not Muslim or Christian, for official purposes, their animism is categorized as a form of Hinduism, which is practically nonexistent in Borneo. Its basic idea is that the dead are not really dead and are able and eager to communicate with us, and we are not really alive, and this is not the only world, but a dream, which is typical of Brazilian anthropologist Viveiros de Castro's "indigenous multiperspectivism," and flies in the face of the Western rational scientific view that this is the real world, and the only one there is. But even the cosmologist and theoretical physicist Stephen Hawking said recently, "One day there may be proof of multiple universes." This world, middle-earth, where the Dayak dwell, arose out of a cosmic battle in the beginning of time between a primal couple, a male and female bird/dragon (serpent). They end up committing mutual, procreative murder, and the present universe arose, stage by stage, from their body parts.

I have collected myths of origin, animal fables, beliefs in ghosts and the supernatural, and cosmological structures in many different cultures, and the striking thing is that they all have dramatic validity, they ring true, and speak of the communications that are going on between living things all the time on many different levels, most audibly and intensely and riotously in rain forests. All these animal and spirit alter egos, the complex systems of correspondences and reciprocities with other creatures that many indigenous cultures have, are natural products of identification with prey and their other predators, with birds that sing beautifully, and so on, which humans, all mammals, with their mirror neurons, spindle cells, and other mechanisms of perception and empathy, are hard wired for. In Max Weber's oft-quoted observation, "Man is an animal suspended in webs of significance he himself has spun." These webs are as varied and inventive as there are different cultures, and each of them is valid to the people who are brought up in them. They provide structure and meaning to the events they are living. To me it is self-evident that where a belief system that arose from the local landscape and ecosystem is still in effect, it is valid and real and has to be respected. Dinétah, the land of the Navajo, for instance, is a very different reality, a parallel universe from the rest of America. You feel this the moment you enter it.

The Penan cosmos is more complicated than Western depictions of Hindu Kaharingan, the religion that all of Kalimantan's "Dayaks" are supposed to have (although it is Dr. B's impression that the Dayak are juggling seven different layers of reality), or the three-tiered Judeo-Christian one. According to Ian's understanding of it, gleaned from hours of talking with Galang, "There are a number of different lands or worlds, two or three above our heads, depending on how I interpret certain myths, and two below our feet. We live in *tana' lu'*, "our world." The uppermost world is above the dome of the sky. A mythical hero once broke through the dome and reached it, but it is not accessible to humans. There may be another land in the sky, because in one myth, the house of a thunder spirit is said to be in the clouds.

"There are three afterworlds," he said, "and one of these is clearly above our heads—I know this, because souls of the dead can throw fruit down to their relatives. This is the best place, like heaven, and is reserved for the virtuous. Another afterworld is no real improvement on the place we live now. People who are neither good nor bad end up there. Then there is a really bad place, like hell, and since it is a burning forest, I can't rule out that rumors of Christian hell have influenced aspects of it. To get to the first two afterworlds you cross a river; if you're really bad, you get stuck on the near side, where hell is.

"*Tana' lu'*, our own world, contains us and our *sahé*, or 'spirit doubles,' which remain detached from us as long as we live, but act as our souls and go to an afterworld once we're dead. All other living things have only *balei*, the spirits who take care of them. These spirits have freedom, and sometimes move between worlds. Each *balei* constitutes a race, and there are as many of these races as there are kinds of living things and natural phenomena.

"The *sahé* was co-opted by the missionaries and turned into the conventional Christian soul. *Balei* were rebranded as so many devils, and a new word was coined for them—*sitan*—borrowed from *Satan*. Traditionally, spirits were good or bad depending on how you treated them. The missionaries sought to portray them all as pure evil. Rungu [Phyllis Webster] wrote a hymnal for the Penan, in which she invited them to *mejuk kekat sitan* [reject all satans]. Under my influence, Galang now corrects Penans who use the word *sitan* when referring to Penan myths—telling them the correct term is *balei* [spirit]. That is my accomplishment, and I am proud of it.

"Then there are two worlds below our feet," Mackenzie continued. "One you reach by diving into a deep place in the river, where you find a hole into a land that's like ours. The other is reached through the hole of a burrowing cicada. *Balei* live in both these places."

I am eager to hear what Nelson and the others are going to say. Nelson is devoutly Christian and seems to have an inferiority complex about his own culture. But everybody here seems perfectly open and ready to talk about anything. I am not encountering the barriers that are sometimes thrown up by indigenous people, particularly if you ask about their spiritual beliefs. Which is of course what I am most interested in. Usually it takes a while to find common ground and build trust before an indigenous person will talk about his deepest, most private beliefs and thoughts, which are very different from the way we modern Westerners see things. Getting to know a new culture requires time, and knowledge of the language, neither of which we have. I know from experience that the first week's impressions of anywhere new are worthless because you are comparing it to what you know—why, this guy is just like so-and-so back home, and so forth. You have to throw away your preconceptions and get into their time and space. We'll do our best in the time we have, but I am not expecting any major breakthroughs here.

The Yanomami I met in 1976 were juggling thirteen different layers of reality. The Penan, before evangelization, which began in the late 1950s and ended with the conversion of the last, most remote nomadic bands twenty years later, were dealing with nine, but only a few elders are still in communication with them anymore.

"Nobody in our camp knows anything about the eight other *taná* or the many races of *balei*," Nelson assures me. "If there is something they are not comfortable talking about, I will tell you. But they honestly don't know about these things anymore, and neither do I."

Animal Stories

The Penans' *suket*, "myths," explain why the world is the way it is, how its animals and plants came into being, the Penans' place in it, and how they are supposed to behave. These stories are also being forgotten, but Rajah Jamale, Choeling, and Nelson know a few. I am particularly interested in their animal myths. They sound a lot like the Awá's, and the *gano* or "just-so stories" three Babendjele Pygmies sang for me in 2010. There are several *suket* about shape shifting—humans becoming animals and vice versa—which tell you about the particular species they identify with most and the reciprocities and correspondences they have with them.

Nelson explains: "The knowledge about the nature, you can ask every man anywhere, but there is no one who can teach you. Even Penan don't know how to teach you the experience we have. It's so deep," Nelson begins. (I run this by Ian when I get back, and he says, "There is indeed no Penan who can tell you about their 'knowledge of nature,' because the English word *nature* corresponds to no word or concept in the Penan universe. *Nature* is a modern secular concept, a Western idea he's picked up from environmentally tuned-in tourists.")

Nelson continues. It seems to be a performance he has given many times before: "I call myself to the spirit of the nature to come to you and talk to you. The first one in the forest is smell. It can tell you something, and the second one is ear. And third is eye. Tomorrow I will show you how the spirit talk to us. You smell what food is being cooked. The smell of tree fallen, the smell of soil that is new or if animal pissed three hours ago or one. The thing that is for me very interesting is I grow up in forest, we were always moving and doing our daily activity, collecting fruit. We see wind moving leaves on mountain. I can remember my father walking. Everything that happened in the forest that I experienced, I remember. The forest is full of memories and stories, the forest gives me a free freedom. The most important thing about being in the forest is to look after your own self so there will be no problem. I can smell your durian fruit in plastic bag. What I wish to show you tomorrow is this is not magic but the reality. This kind of ant is living in this kind of rattan. They will start to make a sound, *tchyou tchyou*. Everything has spirit. Tree, palm, animals have a spirit. That is how Penan believe in the past. For bullfrog I don't have any experience of its spirit. I don't have any knowledge about it, but everything have their own spirit, their own god."

A three-inch-long green praying mantis lands on my plate. "There weren't many mantises in Bedford," Davie says. "I don't think I saw more than three or four the whole time I was there."

"They were as rare as luna or cecropia moths," I agree. "Here they're all over the place and much bigger and greener."

Hundreds of ephemerids are swarming the lightbulb in the kitchen. Nelson continues: "The hornbill spirit can make people walk very fast. Normally what takes two to three days to walk, they do it in one. The leopard spirit is even more powerful. You look for some kind of stone in its meat so you can run or jump very fast. Normally for this kind of thing the spirit will talk to them inside their dream."

"How do you get the help of the hornbill spirit?" I ask.

"You find something not normal in a hornbill, you kill it, then you keep it. Then maybe first night, second night, you have dream, so you just follow what the spirit telling you so you have the power." He is careful to add, "But because we are now Christian, we only believe in Lord Jesus. I know there are other spirits, but I do not belong to them anymore." To Nelson there is only one god, and one reality, but "Christians can still see some of the spirits moving that were more important in the past."

"What is your religion?" Nelson asks.

"Well, I come from a family of devout Russian Orthodox, I was brought up Episcopalian, made a minister of the Universal Life Church [in a heated moment in a storefront church in Harlem by my guitar teacher and guru the Reverend Gary Davis, which Davie is amused to learn got me a 4-D discharge from the Marines, the D standing for divinity] and my brother and sister are practicing Tibetan Buddhists, but I'm not much for institutionalized religion. I guess you could say I'm an agnostic animist."

It is only after several days that Nelson, in one of our morning discussions, suddenly grows somber, and tells us about the tragic death of his father, Kelesau Na'an, who was the headman of Long Kerong, and "a big activist in Southeast Asia. Samling was asking illiterate Penan to sign over their forest, and my father put a stop to it. Thirty years ago he walked from the middle to the upper Baram talking to the Penan in each community and telling them you have to organize. When I was still young he told me, I hope you'll become like this cigarette lighter [and ignite the resistance]." Nelson has a photo of his father that was taken in the 1950s. "It was the end of nakedness. The missionaries have arrived. He is wearing clothes. [Although the Penan were never naked; the men wore loincloths and the women skirts of bark cloth. The women's breasts were exposed, but that was not considered to be nudity.] He started blockades more than twenty years ago. We did it almost every month where logging was happening. Three years ago people from Samling came to Long Kerong two or three times asking where is he, where is he going? They wanted to cut our trees but he wouldn't let them. He was last seen alive going to his paddy field to check the animals in their cages. The whole village looked for him for a month. One day one of the men from Long Sepigan, our neighbors, was walking along the path we always take along the Segita River and found his skeleton. There were just a few bones, but his watch was on his wrist and his necklace was around his neck and his *sarung parang* (machete sheath) was near the skeleton. My father knew that path. He walked it thousands of times, even during the night. There was no danger. We believe he has been killed and I hope the whole world will understand our situation. Now we are under the pressure. We want to be free."

On the 28th of November (in our calendar, which is beginning to seem increasingly irrelevant), after raining cats and dogs through the night, the sun comes up over the next ridge into clear blue sky and shines through the gap in the trees, and the forest comes to life. The day shift, that is. We hear a dawn chorus of gibbons down in the valley, rising and falling like some kind of a catcall competition, then the *kerinin*, the crickets, then the six o'clock cicadas start their grating F-sharp drone, which sounds like a circular saw cutting into steel. They do this every day of the year at dawn and dusk. "Rolex? We don't need no stinking Rolex," I think as I lie in my hammock. They are followed by other kinds of cicada with different songs, which get louder as the sun and the heat of the day rise. Asian paradise flycatchers and other birds come in. The morning biophony, *tutti speci*.

Choeling, stoking the fire in her hut, starts to sing a traditional song to the men, which Nelson translates: "Wake up, don't you hear the gibbon? It's time to go hunting. I will stay and prepare to cook what you bring. You wake up in the morning before the clouds rise up in the sky, you are already moving like the leopard, through the hills and mountains. But I am still not prepared for your return."

Sagung and one of the young men, Puh, have already gone off with the dogs and their shotguns. Why not their blowguns? I ask Nelson, and he explains, "They are taking shotguns because they want to make it faster. They don't want to waste time in the forest with you here. If they have the bullet they prefer the shotgun. Some hunters can dart a small animal from thirty to forty meters, but they have to get close because so many trees in the way." Shotguns are quicker and easier, but the ammo costs money and it depletes game. As I have seen with the Mekranoti and the Awá, the adoption of shotguns is a double-edged sword, a Hobson's choice. It sucks you into the money economy.

Breakfast is muntjac or barking deer (there are also greater and lesser mouse deer, and sambar, the largest of Borneo's Cervidae) and a thick, gelatinous, very starchy porridge of sago palm, much like *matoke*, the mush of long green plantains that was the staple in the village in

Uganda where my wife grew up. Everybody is sticking a special wooden utensil with four prongs into the porridge and swirling it and dunking the blob that gloms onto it in venison juice. "This is kind of like dunking pieces of bread in a fondue," Davie says, putting a dollop of it into his mouth. "Pretty tasty, too." Yesterday it was sago porridge with small tree snails. "You can call barking deer with bamboo whistle," Nelson says. "Or wait by fruiting tree."

"These guys are still doing it," I say to Davie. "They're taking what's useful from the modern world and having nothing to do with the rest. Every item of modern material culture they adopt is a conscious decision. The young mothers have disposable diapers, which means that they have some cash and are in contact with the Western consumer culture, probably in Long Bedian, and are not yet aware of the trash factor of nonbiodegradable 'excrement of oil' products, as Norman Mailer called plastics, that they're being sucked into what Pope Francis calls 'the culture of waste.' They're in control of their lives, except the loggers are cutting the trees in the forest at will, and their schoolgirls are being raped. They're free. You can't keep people like this in zoos. But you can protect their habitat and let them adopt what they want in their own way and due time. Survival International's president, Stephen Corry, has a great book called *Tribal Peoples for Tomorrow's World*, which spells out how vulnerable tribal people are to the seductions of the modern world, how we should be acting in situations like this. But I don't think we have to worry about these people so much. They have already seen what the modern world has to offer and made their choices. They have flashlights, a radio, disposable diapers, cocoa, flip-flops, and cleated sneakers, shotguns, Western clothing. I'm not going to lecture them about the disposable diapers, but at least they keep them from washing shitty diapers in the stream."

"What a great way to be living!" Davie says. "This is what we were trying to do when we were kids in the woods. I guess that's why I feel so at home."

Several black songbirds with forked tails—drongos of some kind—come to check us out, landing in the treetops above us. I ask about the clouded leopard. There are still some, but not many. Sagung killed one last year. He is wearing one of its incisors around his neck. "Python is everywhere, in the forest and in the rivers," Nelson says. "They catch them near here. Sagung's father-in-law had a python wrapped around his leg. It tried to kill him but luckily he had his *parang*."

Choeling chimes in with a long, Freudian just-so story about the snake. "All of Penan women not allowed to eat python in past," she begins (Nelson is translating). "One day a couple goes hunting in forest. On way catch python. Man kills and smokes python over fire. He tells his wife, you can cook it here but don't eat it, and he leaves her to continue hunting. She rolls some sago flour and bakes it into bread. Fat from python drips on the sago *piong* [bread] and she eats it and it's delicious. This is why you ask me not to eat, because you want to eat it all, the woman thinks about her husband. The women gets itchy and everywhere she scratches becomes pattern of python and in the end her whole body becomes a python, and at this moment she remembers what her husband told her, but it's too late. Husband finds her curled up in the kitchen with still human head and scolds her, 'That's why I told you not to eat the python.'

"'The only thing you can do now,' said the woman, 'is to put me into a basket and take me down to the big pool in the river and leave me there and don't look back.' As he walks away he hears *tum tum tum*, the women's head turning into python's. Python's name *redomalui* means 'transformed woman.' Today women are able to eat the python. There is no taboo."

A classic *suket*. The first one Ian Mackenzie heard was the first one Galang told him, fifteen years ago, about the human transformability of the *babui*, the "wild pig." "A man speared a wild pig, which fled, wounded. He tracked it to a pond, which it forded; but on the far side of the water there were only human footprints. The man followed these, and found himself in a village where pigs resume their human shape." Ian knows other *suket* about animals who were originally humans, like the peacock and the coucal who tattoo each other, "but I suspect their human forms are just a gimmick to allow tattooing of smooth skin," he tells me. Nelson also has elaborate dragon tattoos on his upper arms and torso, by the same Bidayuh master who did Sagung's. Sagung explains, "Before gibbon was human. Now it has longer arms than legs. It's upside down. Like human it has no tail because the part where its tail would be was its head, but was cut off by its enemy."

"But there is no generalized tradition of animals descending from people," Ian emphasizes. "The converse exists in two cases: There are two mythical ancestors of humans, one of which is an animal and the other a spirit animal—crocodile and tiger, respectively. According to their *suket*, they were brothers, and had a Penan father and an evil Berawan mother. To escape from their mother they metamorphosed. That means Penans can invoke either of these dangerous creatures, reminding them that they are relatives. They used to do this before hazarding a river crossing. But nowadays there are no crocodiles [in the headwaters of the Baram River system]. Neither Galang nor his brother had ever seen one until I took them to the Miri Zoo."

There isn't as much fluidity between humans and animals as there is in other animistic societies because to the Penan there is a fundamental difference between them: only humans have souls, or *sahé*. Animals have *balei*, or "spirits." Then there are the ghosts, the *beruen,* the people who were so bad their *sahé* don't go anywhere. The Penan, even though they are mostly devout Christians now and the *balei* have pretty much faded out of the picture, still live in fear of the *beruen*.

The Penans' Unique Sign Language

The hunters have returned. Sagung has a big dead *babui* slung over his shoulders. Puh has four dead silverleaf monkeys (so named because they like to eat young leaves with silvery undersides, they are langurs, also known as silvered leaf monkeys), and a live infant, who is lashed to a post of Sagung's hut and is looking in horror and deep sorrow at his parents' bodies thrown on the sapling floor next to him, which Sagung's wife proceeds to butcher, while Rajah guts the pig, scooping the copious amount of blood and innards into a plastic tub. Then the five animals are roasted in their skin and smoked on a big fire Sagung makes in the middle of the camp. Food for everybody for the next few days, except for me and Varial, who are vegetarians.

Davie is amazed how the hunters have come back as neat and clean as when they left, "while I am all smeared and scratched and I haven't even hardly set foot in the forest yet. I was bathing in the stream that runs under the road when they returned with the monkeys and the *babui*, and I'm still dirtier than they are."

After lunch and a nap, Davie, Varial, Nelson, and I, along with Sagung and some of the kids, including Christina, set out into the forest. We are going to find Rajah and the other kids who have gone ahead and left us messages in the special sign language, using branches and leaves, the Penan have for keeping each other apprised of their whereabouts. Each community has its own signs. The Ba Marong have about a hundred. We wade into the mixed dipterocarp forest above the camp. Most of the trees are maybe sixty feet tall, six to ten inches in diameter, sheathed in smooth gray bark spotted with luminous green bull's-eyes of lichen. They look like the same species, but are actually not; there is so much biodiversity in Borneo that different species fill the same niche—the species diversity overwhelms the niche diversity.

There are no emergent dipterocarps in the woods anymore, except for a towering white *gita* (*A. pneumatophora*) whose wood is too soft to be of interest to the logging companies. All we find are the rotting stumps of *meranti*, *kapur*, *kerning*, *nyatoh*, and *zupater*, which were cut down when the road on this ridge was put in from 1991 to 1993. Twenty years later the forest has still not recovered, which supports the contention of antilogging activists that "selective logging" is very destructive, especially on thin-soiled ridgetops and their steep sides. Jimmy says it destroys 60 percent of the forest. No new monarchs have emerged to take the felled trees' places. This forest is a shadow of its former self, a degraded secondary forest, but in the little undisturbed ravines that we climb in and out of as we ascend the ridgecrest, a tangle of corkscrew vines and fig trees drip over the rock like wax from melted candles. It is still the emerald forest.

"This *pulau* in Malay, or *lebung* in Penan, is one of the last islands of small forest left," Nelson explains. "A *pulau* is an island or an area that is distinct from surrounding region. This is Pulau Toking Ja'au—literally 'big mountain island.' *Ba* means 'creek' or 'river,' and *Marong* is a proper name. The Marong River is down below."

Rajah has left us a message: a branch bending slightly up to the right—the direction they have taken. Sagung's ten-year-old daughter has brought the infant *olong* silverleaf monkey with her and is cuddling him and showering him with affection. He seems decidedly less traumatized, to be forgetting his parents, who are in everybody's stomachs, and imprinting on his new furless caregivers. Stockholm syndrome, it seems, is not confined to humans. Nothing is.

The next sign points straight: a branch with crossed leaves in its cut fork, meaning there are two others, both family members, with me. The next sign is a larger cross of sticks in a split sapling, whose right side has a series of cuts: hurry, don't waste time. Next a sapling in whose crotch is a big leaf rolled up into a cup: we are thirsty. With most Penan kids living in modern longhouses and going to school, they aren't learning their community's signs. Just the way the *suket* are losing out to TV, cell phones, and Facebook. "This sign language has to be recorded before it is lost," I tell Nelson. "There is nothing like it anywhere else in the world, as far as I know. The only way to save your forest is to save your culture, and people like us who want to help you will be fascinated to learn of its existence."

A branch cut into four prongs, like a sago porridge swirler, leads us to a sago palm, which another sign declares has been molonged, dibsied by Rajah Jamale, so it's okay for us to eat. Sagung hacks down the multiple stems with pinnate leaflets and cuts out a section of its yellowish white heart and passes around chopped up pieces of it. Unbelievably delicious. The best palmito I have ever had. Ambrosial. Davie agrees. "Eat your heart out, Anthony Bourdain," I tell Varial's camera.

Nelson shows me the contraceptive plant I asked about. "Penan girls marry at around twenty but are free to have sex before," he explains. "This plant makes it impossible to get pregnant forever. We don't show to young women, but woman with five kids who doesn't want more takes it.

"This is medicine for snake, scorpion, millipede bite. Slice and boil root in two spoons of water and drink and wrap piece of root where bite is. Cobra, viper, black-and-yellow-ringed snake, there are more than a dozen poisonous snakes. Snakes live in shadows. Sometimes they go into sun to shed skin. This big leaf is *macaranga*, for roof. They mostly growing in secondary forest." As we walk on, Nelson continues, "This is for headache. The juice of this twisted corkscrew vine is good for soap to wash. The woods of this *poelaio* tree is best for furniture."

Next sign: a bunch of leaves stuffed in the crook of a branch—they are waiting for us. The kids who loved it in the beginning, a new game, have gotten bored and gone ahead, following Rajah's trail.

Sagung finds an agarwood tree and cuts out a yard-long section of its mold-blackened pith, from which the perfume agar, esteemed in China and India for thousands of years, is extracted. Varial thinks it has a granny smell, of rooms with eau de cologne. Davie finds it has a little muskiness, like patchouli, but "is something new I don't have a word for yet." The best-grade agarwood, super one, fetches thirty thousand ringgit ($10,000) per kilo. Medium is ten thousand ringgit. Good money. Sagung will spend hours over the next few days sitting in his hut digging out the black part from slabs he brought back, when he is not whittling darts for his blowpipe. One of the main reasons for the relative rarity and high cost of agarwood is that there is very little left in the wild. It's listed by CITES (the Convention on International Trade in Endangered Species) as an Appendix II, "potentially threatened," species.

At last we reach the top of the ridge. We find Rajah and the kids sitting in a *jamin* that they have thrown up and thatched with palm. "People like us would really like to learn how you build these huts," I tell Nelson.

Davie says, "I don't think I've had such a great time in the woods since when we were kids," and I ask, "Remember the time we built a fire and you dug some white grubs out the pith of a rotting maple log with your pocketknife and said, 'I hear the Indians eat these things and they're really good,' so we roasted 'em and popped 'em into our mouths, and they were scrumptious?" Davie doesn't remember this. But for me, it was like a foretaste of the wild food foraging trips I would tag along with in the Amazon, and the greasy winged termites I would eat with Efe Pygmies in the Ituri Forest.

"This sago palm heart"—I bite into another chunk—"it's so clean and pure and refreshing. I don't even know what to compare it to."

"You're right, Panda," Davie says. "It don't get any better than this. We've returned to the imaginary jungle of our childhood. It's like we've come full circle."

"Hey, let's have a contest," I tell Nelson. "See who can do the best animal imitation and I'll give a prize to the winner." Everybody thinks this is a great idea. Christina does a spot-on gibbon call. Her dad, Sagung, does a tour de force helmeted hornbill, its whole call repertoire; Rajah does a rhinoceros hornbill; Puh shows us how a *babui* roots and grunts and bursts from the underbrush on all fours. Nelson climbs a tree and swings from one vine to another like a short-tailed macaque. They're all great. It's impossible to determine the winner. Back in camp, I decide to divide the performances into four categories, and end up giving a prize to everybody: extra shirts, shorts, flashlight, everything I can spare.

When we return from the forest, three men from Long Si'ang, the next Penan community further out on the ridge, are waiting to see us. They have a detailed map of their customary forest land, but Shin Yang, one of the logging companies, is preparing to log in it. The company says it has a government license. The three men want us to bring international attention to this injustice and help them stop it. The Melfra Keng logging company says it has a government license to log in Ba Marong. Davie and I have seen a smartly dressed management-type Chinese man in a new pickup driving back and forth during our long walks on the road along the ridge. He is from Melfra Keng, and is waiting for us to leave so he can talk to Sagung about coming in and doing the second cut, which Sagung is not going to let happen. The Ba Marong and the Penan of Long Si'ang really have their backs to the wall.

The next morning, Saturday, November 30, we awaken to insect, bird, and human chatter rejoicing in being alive. Another day has dawned, and the women are laughing to each other, saying, "Now that Varial has taken your picture and wants to keep it, he will fall in love with you." They are all saying he is mine, no he is mine. I say they should have seen *me* thirty years ago. They say even old is okay. Now they are fighting over me. The language is very musical. The women let out fast staccato rhythmic strings of syllables, *huma tara tara tate*. As with Pygmies, there is no difference between music and speech. I play and sing "How Great Thou Art," which they know.

"They have a sense of humor about our being here with them," Varial says. "Now they are open. They understand where we are coming from and they want to play. And now we have to go." Jimmy is supposed to be coming for us in three days.

Rajah comes over with his blowpipe and bamboo poison-dart container, which he opens. It contains not only darts but a jaw harp, on which his wife, Akons, gives a bravura performance, playing up a storm on the world's first and oldest musical instrument. This one is exquisitely carved from a single piece of wood. The wood is hard and inflexible, and the labellum is long and thin, like the style of a female flower.

When she has finished, Nelson explains why men keep the instrument in their dart container: "Sometimes they get lost, and bad spirits come out of dead branches in the trees, and you play it for a very long time, until the spirits have no time to go with you anymore and move on."

Sagung is sitting cross-legged in his hut shaving darts with a special knife from slivers of *jakah* palm. "You have to choose *jakah* with fruits or it is not strong enough," Nelson explains. "They have always hunted with dogs. The spear is used if animal is close to them. The pipe of the *nyagang*, 'blowpipe,' is very hard. Bore must be dead straight or you miss. How make pipe? Prepare piece of wood. Stand up pipe, make hole with iron rod. Clean hole with sago palm roots. They can borrow iron bore from other group in this area. Most of time you are shooting monkeys or birds up in trees."

Rajah has a milky left eye, which he lost the sight of in an accident twenty-three years ago. "Don't ask what happened," Nelson says. "It's not polite to say you notice." But when we tack a square of cardboard on a tree sixty feet away, Rajah nails it with his dart three times in a row. I try it and the third time hit the square myself. Varial tries and doesn't do as well, and Davie, with one arm, watches. No one asks how he lost his other arm or draws the slightest attention to it, and Davie is so dignified and speaks in such a gentle, soothing voice, and is always thinking of the rest of us and never complaining and saying *jian kenin* all the time, and the all-purpose word for *thank you* and *all is good*, *kwa kwa*, he reminds Rajah and Nelson of Rajah Brooke, the three generations of perfect gentlemen who treated the Orang Ulu kindly and fairly and left them alone. Davie tells me for years after his arm was ripped off when his snowmobile overturned, he experienced excruciating phantom limb pain, but in 2009 he had an operation on the nerves in his shoulder, whose odds of success were slim, and it worked, and now he doesn't even know it isn't there. He has learned to work around it, like Rajah Jamale with his blind eye. Later I will read that people with phantom limb pain are supposed to be more compassionate, to feel others' pain better, because they don't have the "that's not me" reaction most of us do. But Davie was always compassionate, long before he lost his arm.

Sagung tells a *suket* about the crocodile and the leopard while the dogs are curled up in the still warm ashes of the monkey and pig roast. "One couple has two sons," he says. "Man is Penan, woman is *va'e*, from another tribe. This family live alone in the forest. The sons are too young, playing around hut. Mother prepares food but not the right food, not good food for them. There is dirt in it. They eat it and feel itchy. One's skin gets small bubbles like the skin of crocodile, other's skin has lots of spots like leopard. The two kids go down to the river after father left for hunting. They decide to have a contest: who can jump to other side becomes a leopard and one who doesn't make it becomes crocodile. Older brother becomes leopard, younger becomes crocodile. They talk to each other, our mother bad to us, and agree when she goes to deep place in the river to bathe, crocodile will eat. From today on we are allowed to attack any *va'e* person. They agree crocodile will leave part of mother on branch for leopard. One day when leopard walking near river crocodile tries to catch him but he is too fast. Leopard says you breaking our agreement and crocodile says from now on I will not attack anything unless I make sure it is *va'e*. But some Penan are attacked because they do not touch food when offered and don't want. If you don't eat something that you are offered you will have *tingen*, 'bad luck,' a crocodile will eat you or a snake will bite you. If you don't join others to eat, even when you don't have time to stay, it is better to at least taste the food so you don't have *tingen*." This seems to be a variant of the tiger/crocodile origin myth.

Were humans here first? I ask. "No," Sagung says. "Only some animals like gibbons are transformed humans. The others were here just as long. The difference is that animals have *balei* and humans have *sahé*. If you are a good person you listen to your *sahé* and let it guide you, you will rejoin it when you die." Where is Choeling's *sahé*? I ask, and she says, "I don't have one because I am in the modern world." Edwin, our cook, the aspiring architect, is taking notes beside me as I scribble away. He sees the importance of getting all this down for future generations.

Davie and Varial and I are finally beginning to settle into the time and space of where we are, progressing beyond the "this is just like" stage, because this is like nothing else. Christina writes in beautiful penmanship in my notebook:

Bé' akeu jam surat: "I don't know how to read and write."

I say to Davie, "This girl could go anywhere if she had the chance. She's got it all. But she isn't even going to school anymore. It's too dangerous with the loggers raping girls on their way to school, or giving them a few ringgit to have sex. I wonder how her life is going to turn out. Sagung doesn't think the modern world has much to offer. He hasn't even taken her to Miri."

"The loggers come," Nelson says, translating for him. "The Penan don't know about cigarettes, wine, and all this bullshit thing, and start doing bad things like changing dress, steal like Mafia, have accident by car or motorbike. The modern world bring hell on Earth, but you can't stop it."

A huge *tekenyit*, "dragonfly," zips through. There is no *suket* for dragonfly, but a human who is moving around all the time, zipping from place to place, can be a *tekenyit*. You and I are *tekenyit*, I tell Varial. Maybe we should change the name of our *Suitcase on the Loose* show.

The hunters bring in a small barking deer and a *bekuleu*, a "leopard cat" (*P. bengalensis*) that they have killed with their blowguns. There are ten kinds of spotted cat here, the largest being the cloud leopard. The Penans' main relationship with their fellow creatures is not mystical but food. The silent scream of the silverleaf monkey being barbecued yesterday does not have the grotesque horror for them that it did for us.

Flames are dancing around the black pot in which the venison is being cooked with cabbage and onion. Shafts of sunlight with insects coming and going are breaking through the rising wood smoke.

I write a song to the tune of "How Great Thou Art":

we are the Penan
we live in the forest
and we don't take any more than what we need
the forest gives us food and medicine
it gives us everything we need

we don't need your money
because we got honey
we don't want your dams drying up our rivers
we don't need your chain saws cutting down our trees
we don't want your pollution or diseases
all we want is to be left alone in the forest that gives us life
all we want is to live free in our own land
all we want is to be Penan
this is the land of our fathers
not the land of the loggers
this is the land of our sons and daughters

Nelson translates it but it doesn't work in Penan. It's very hard to put it into the Penan sensibility and the sound and flow of their language.

"The kids are playing in the forest like we did," Davie observes, "but there's a lot of control because there is respect which trickles down all the way to the dogs in this camp, this multicultural multispecies ecosystem. It's such a treat to be with all these other beings, the cicadas' psychedelic didgeridoo, the crickets' shaman rattle. The pigs are rooting, the dogs are snoozing, the bees are buzzing, the women are weaving, the men are cutting out agarwood, the kids are playing in the woods, in the camp, it doesn't matter."

"We have become children again," Varial says when he comes back from the stream where he was playing with the kids. He has flowers in the rattan headband Choeling wove for him.

The six o'clock cicadas announce the beginning and the end of the day. This is their role in the daily biophony of the animal orchestra. After six p.m. two other species of cicada come in, taking us and so many other forms of life into the darkness, when a whole other suite of animals, the night shift, will take over while we sleep. That's when the real action happens—after dark. That's when most of the species, which have been laying during the day, insects camouflaged as leaves or twigs, snakes and frogs hiding in the shadows, spring into action.

December 2—I think that's the date—it was raining cats and dogs all night, and the six o'clock cicadas are ten minutes late. The forest floor that was drying out is muddy and slippery again. I make a big speech.

I have one more present for Choeling for best dancer and making all the beautiful bracelets for us. Choeling has woven five bracelets from the black inner pith of rattan for each of us. "You have to do it for yourselves," I begin. "You need a business person to make you money so you don't have to sell bushmeat or agarwood to the Kayan. You must *molong*, preserve your culture. You can only save your forest if your culture is strong. This century is the battle for the planet, for the last rain forest, for human rights, particularly women and girls' right to be educated and to be equal." I give Nelson the copy of *I am Malala* that I brought to read on the plane and inscribe it, "May you become the Malala of the Penan and their cigarette lighter."

"What we can do," I tell the Ba Marong, "is document your life here and show the world how beautiful it is."

Varial takes a portrait of each member of the band, holding the message they want to send to the world written on a page from my notebook. We are not telling them how to pose or what to wear, but they decide themselves how they want the world to see them. They are looking serious and proud and humble straight into the camera against a screen of banana leaves and palm fronds that Varial, who has done a lot of fashion shoots in Montreal, has set up. Each comes one by one. Even the toddlers, with the help of their parents and the girl who is still scared of us, stand alone holding their message. Puh, who has been dressed smartly in a yellow Liverpool soccer shirt and matching knee socks, has chosen to be photographed in his traditional loincloth, holding his blowgun.

A sampling of the twenty-three messages: *My forest is safe, I'm happy; I'm happy because my forest is still there; I'm angry because my forest is being destroyed; I need to protect the forest for my children and grandchildren so they will have a good life forever; Give me a fan to keep the flies away* [the flies are the loggers]*; I am sick because I drink dirty water; I make a blockade because the logging is bad.*

Then Varial and Davie and I are photographed, in the spirit of the new collective anthropology, where the ethnographers become objects of study themselves. Varial's message: *I am the son of the forest. Protect the forest.* Me, in big caps: *MOLONG.* Davie: *The Penan demonstrate in their actions and lifestyle the most important values the human race possesses. They reach out to us today. I am grateful for their example.*

December 3. Day eleven. Everybody's getting a little restless. Nobody is going to be staying here; they've given us a taste of their life in the forest and are eager to get back to their lives. Rajah and his wife are all packed, and two of his other sons come on motorbikes and take them away. Where is Jimmy? He was supposed to come yesterday.

The three of us are getting a little cynical. To what extent has this camp been a Potemkin village thrown up for our sake, and for theirs? But it doesn't matter, because their love of the forest, and the imminent danger it's in, are real. They can't be blamed for adapting to the modern world, which they didn't ask to come into their lives. And in a way they are still nomadic, moving between their forest camps and the modern longhouses and hanging out in Long Bedian. They're seminomadic and semisettled. But they still have the mentality of forest nomads, and the hunting and gathering skills, and they're feeding themselves from the bounty of the forest. After some discussion we decide to give each of the twenty-three of them thirty ringgit, ten bucks apiece from each of us. You're not supposed to do this with indigenous people. Survival International would not approve. This creates a culture of dependency and hastens the demise of the traditional culture. (Like the Dogon of Mali. They used to carve amazing wooden statues, but when I visited them in 2003 the younger generation was hustling sleeping bags and headlamps they bummed off tourists. But now, with the Al Qaeda of the Maghreb having taken over much of Mali, there is no tourism to Dogon country. I wonder what young Dogon are doing to make ends meet.) But the Ba Marong are no longer traditional. They are transitional, and belong to the money culture; as entry-level members, they can use the money. Sagung says he wants to build a modern longhouse to establish the Ba Marong's customary presence here. So we have contributed $690 to the cause.

Davie and I walk several miles on the ridge we came up on and where Jimmy was supposed to have come for us yesterday. The Chinese guy passes us both ways but doesn't stop to pick us up even though we flag him down. He has us pegged as outside agitators and is waiting for us to leave so he can pressure Sagung to let his company come in and do the second cut.

Davie and I talk about Bedford, how neither of us, nor many of our contemporaries, ended up going along with the drill and becoming part of the old American Establishment. "I regret letting down my heritage and my parents, who were wonderful," Davie says. "Dad was a real man of the fifties type guy, and I didn't live up to his expectations. But at the end—he died in 2002—we reconciled. I remember when I went out west in 1967 and never came back. I went into a pawnshop in Colorado and traded my Bass Weejuns and white collared shirts for a pair of work boots and coveralls. Eisenhower sure was right when he warned America about the perils of the military-industrial complex. Look at us now. Look at this. Its reach is everywhere. No place is safe anymore."

We're still strong enough to walk four or five miles in the blazing equatorial sun, dredging up deeply buried memories, not all of them happy, and stopping to poke around in the woods just like old times.

When we get back to the camp, Jimmy has arrived. He has brought a huge sign that he had made in Miri—the reason for his delay, as it wasn't ready till yesterday—and puts it up on the side of the road, right across from our camp. It says:

REFORESTATION OF PENAN OF BA MARONG
SECURITY FOOD LIVELIHOOD AND NATURAL ENVIRONMENT

along with an impressive list of international sponsors with their logos, including the International Union for Conservation of Nature (IUCN), the National Sustainable-Forestry Committee of The Netherlands, and the World Conservation Union. Hopefully this will act as a deterrent. It's about all he can do. The police don't arrest wood poachers, he explains. "They have already stolen a lot of wood. This Chinese guy has a license. He will come in anyway."

Jimmy has also brought a GPS map he made of Ba Marong that he gives to Sagung. In 1962 the British asked all the natives to demarcate their communal boundaries. Those along the Baram River itself did:

Penan, Kenyah, Kelabit, and Kayan. But many of these highland *taná* still need to be mapped.

Everybody, including the dogs and the pigs, comes down to say good-bye. The animals will join the Ba Marong at their next camp; meanwhile there still are a lot of pickings at this emptying one. The boys bring down our gear and as we are loading it in the back of Jimmy's Mitsubishi, the Chinese guy pulls up in his.

I have distributed some last presents: three polo shirts, one head-lamp, a pen flashlight, and a folding knife. Choeling has given us her beautifully woven rattan bracelets, and we all have Penan names. Varial is Kiget: he's always moving, looking for a picture. I am Lakei Nyape, always playing my guitar. Davie is honored with the name Lakei Penan (you are Penan, a Penan Man). The same name their nomadic cousins gave to Bruno Manser, who lived with them for six years and became their champion. Davie has the kindness, gentleness, humility, and dignity that are esteemed in their society.

Shopping in Long Bedian

The next day, after spending the night again at Long Karavan, we stop for lunch in Long Bedian, the trading center for the Middle Baram. There we find Sagung, wearing a second watch on his wrist (neither to keep track of the time with) and four of the young women, sporting new pink tights and disco bags. After we left, the Chinese guy in the truck gave a lift to all of them who didn't go on motorcycles. He is offering a hundred ringgit to each of them for letting Melfra Keng come in with bulldozers and chain saws and do the second cut. Sagung is not interested. There's no commercial timber left on the ridge, so they must be talking about down in the valley across the road, where the men went hunting each morning. The slope down to the valley floor is very steep. Getting the trees out is going to do a lot of collateral damage. One hundred ringgit is three bucks more than we gave each of the twenty-three of them. That should put the Chinese guy's offer into perspective and make it clear that there are alternatives to letting what is left of their *taná* be destroyed.

Speaking of money, which we have a relatively unlimited supply of, we lay on provisions for the next leg of our journey: coffee, ten kilos of rice, toilet paper, lentils, one carton menthol Era cigs, two lighters, evaporated milk, two bars soap, cookies, peanuts, eggs. Long Bedian has a Wild West frontier feel. In one shop there is an electric *sape*, the stringed instrument we will soon be hearing played by one of its masters, as well as a hornbill casque, a bear claw, and a switchblade knife. Another, where the girls got their new outfits, has the latest women's fashions. Varial has red spots from sand flies and an infection on his ankle from playing Tarzan and swinging through the treetops during our animal imitation contest. Neosporin isn't doing much for it, so I start him on a dose of amoxicillin.

We continue northwest, toward the eastern border of Mulu National Park, and cross, on a raised road, the natural gas pipeline put in a few years ago from Sabah to the port of Bintulu, down the Sarawak coast from Miri. A huge gash going over hill and dale, the pipeline has a service road along which some of the last seminomadic Penan have been persuaded to settle in shantytowns and longhouses.

Radu

We arrive in the rain at Long Mara'am, (or Mera'an), a community of several hundred people on the Mago River. Long Mara'am is on the other side of the Mago and can only be reached by a suspension bridge just wide enough for dirt bikes, which there is a steady procession of, tooling around on them being the teenagers' favorite thing to do. Several of them ferry our stuff across for the three days Jimmy is leaving us here. The new community consists of several dozen freestanding houses, built in a variety of styles, some ramshackle shacks, a few well-built two-story structures with gardens and fences, most with metal roofs, ranged around a big square at the front side of which is a church. The original longhouse, built by the logging company that cleared the route of the pipeline, burned down four years ago. The Penan of Long Mara'am had blockaded the pipeline three times. The fourth time the state ministry in charge of pipeline routes negotiated a settlement of 250,000 ringgit. Hence all the dirt bikes, and the electric guitars and big amps and speakers in the church. Their previous village, which a church with glass windows stood in the middle of, was nearby. Mackenzie visited it in 1994. Before that, they were nomadic. Three aging households are still seminomadic. They roam in nearby Mulu Park, whose eastern border is a day in from here. This is what is left of the band that Bruno Manser lived with three decades ago.

A hydro dam is planned on the upper Tutoh, a tributary of the Baram that the Mago runs into. The dam is one of eight planned for the Baram system. This is the next phase of the rape of Sarawak. Radu, the master *sape* player I have come to see and hear and jam with, says Long Mara'am will be flooded out. He is not sure where they will go when that happens. Radu is in his fifties, about the same age as Rajah Jamale, an elder and like him a former headman whose son is now the headman. We stay in Radu's son's house, which has a big room with a television and a little freezer full of cold drinks, a little store, a kitchen, and a laundry, shower, and outhouse in back. Radu's place, fifty yards away, is more modest.

His *sape* is leaning against one of the walls of the big room. The long, slender body of the stringed instrument is made from the soft, light white wood of the *gita* tree. The neck and the large rectangular body, left open and facing the back, are carved from a single piece. Tuning pegs are fixed to either side of the neck, and on the soundboard little bridges, on which five strings are stretched, have been placed at various intervals. The strings span more than three octaves, but only the top one is used to play the melody. The others are drone strings, like the Indian sitar, which the *sape* is thought to be descended from. The lute of the Orang Ulu, particularly the Kenyah and Kayan, the *sape* was originally restricted to ritualistic music to induce trance, but in the last century it gradually became a social instrument to accompany dances or to provide entertainment on its own, or in *sape* string bands. This *sape* is electrified, like one we saw for sale in Long Bedian. Radu is the last player in Long Mara'am. The younger generation listens to Malay rap and disco and plays the electric guitars and drum sets in the church. There is an annual Rainforest World Music Festival outside Kuching that attracts many of the best *sape* players, but Radu has never been. And some of the jungle lodges have *sape* players who serenade the tourists like mariachi bands in Mexico or ukulele strummers on Hawaii.

Radu has a repertoire of twenty or so minor-sounding major pentatonic runs that he plays up and down the fretboard of the instrument
with his thumb, while hitting the drone strings contrapuntally like the
fifth string of a banjo. It sounds totally Appalachian, but the pentatonic
is found in the music of every culture, and Radu says he plays the *sape*
to express his love for the forest, and that he learned his melodies from
the birds.

"Behind the Christian god of the missionaries is our own god, Balei Pu'un," he explains, with Nelson translating. "The world was not
created by Balei Pu'un. It was already there. His job is to help people
be good to each other. The way he communicates is through a bird
or animal, because people cannot see him, so he needs a translator, a
special person who is able to understand animals. My father was one of
these people, and he taught me how to do it. Balei Pu'un uses two kinds
of bird, *kemiok* and *pip bukang*." He imitates their call: 1–2–3–4–5,
same note.

"This is not the real world," Radu goes on. How do you get to the
real world? I ask. "Only those who have good habits can go there. Bad
people will stay in the air. To enter the real world you have to die." This
sounds to me like the Hindu Kaharingan of the Dayaks in Kalimantan.

Ian Mackenzie says Balei Pu'un is a "euphemism, a simplification
for Western monotheistic consumption. There is no supreme being."
Nelson and Radu talked about Balei Pu'un because the *balei* (the ones
who weren't turned into *sitan*, "demons") have been assimilated into
the Christian Lord God. Mackenzie explains, "The Penan have no word
in their language for *god*, there is no named demiurge or creator god.
If you ask them today if *Balei Pu'un* is one or more spirits, most of
them will say one, but in fact it refers to many different races of spirits.
Galang tells me that *balei pu'un* is an alternative name for *balei kenan-
gan*, the spirits that sustain people and give us life."

"Can we hear Balei Pu'un speaking through an animal in the forest?" I ask Radu.

"If I hear something, I will let you know. We can go to the forest,
but we can't be sure anything will happen." Is there a best time of day?
"No time of day is better. If it happens, it happens." Has Balei Pu'un
told him what he feels about people cutting trees, building dams, and
destroying the forest home of Penan, and what to do about it? Has

Radu received any message from Balei Pu'un that he is not happy? "No, but Balei Pu'un teaches Penan to look after the area, so they are responsible for their part of the forest." So what to do to stop the destruction? "We don't know how. We are only telling loggers you can't cut the trees. We have houses and settlements in the forest. It is most important to let us live in our *tana'*. But we will not kill or hurt them."

What will happen to Balei Pu'un if the forest is gone? "He will try to find another place where there is still forest." What if there is no more forest in the whole world? "We don't know, but yah, it could be the end of the world." Like the Awá's "cosmic famine."

"Compared to other people we are very poor, but we receive people and give them what we have," Radu continues. "If a few thousand people want to have more and more, they have to understand without *molong* there is nothing left. This is the only way to save the world." I wonder, again, how much of this sentiment is Radu, and how much the more acculturated Nelson's translation.

One afternoon a marvelous-looking Penan man steps out of the forest. He has long black hair and rings of woven black rattan pith on his upper arms and calves and is the most authentic-looking Penan we have met yet, despite his soccer shorts and plastic flip-flops. His striking face is creased with humor, and his name is Asik Nyelit. I don't realize it, and won't until Jimmy tells me when he picks us up, but Asik is the headman of the Baubung, the nomadic band Bruno Manser lived with for six years, from 1984 to 1990. They are on the river Ubong, about a day's walk into the high mountainous forest from here, and are still seminomadic, more so than the Ba Marong. There are no true nomads, or *jepens*, left. The last ones were settled in 2008, along the access road of the pipeline that was built through their *tana'*.

Long Mara'am, in fact, split from the Baubung. It was founded by Radu's father in the late 1980s, with members of the band who didn't want to be nomads anymore. Asik still comes here with sago flour and meat from the forest to trade for modern goods and to visit with his cousins, the reason for this trip.

Asik produces a jaw harp and a nose flute and plays both virtuosically. I trade a beaded necklace I picked up in Long Bedian for two of his bracelets, one of small white glass beads in circular threaded clusters of eight, the other of cross-woven white and orange plastic, and add them to Choeling's rattan bangle and the silver loop from a melted colonial five-franc piece I picked up in Antananarivo, Madagascar, in 1986 and have been wearing on my left wrist ever since. Asik returns to the forest some time later and I will not see him again. A year and a half later, I am still wearing the two bracelets I traded him for. Every time I look at them, they remind me of the Penan and how we have to intensify the fight for their forest. I will wear them to my grave.

"When you think there are seven billion of us *orang asing* and so few of us have visited these wonderful people," Davie muses as we watch dirt bikes crisscrossing the vast central courtyard in the rain the next morning from the porch of the chief's house. All night long peals of thunder echoed in the mountains, and there were sporadic downpours. A front has moved in.

The rain stops. Here comes Radu. He wishes to say something. He is happy we ask him all these questions. Our coming here was a surprise. It was interesting that we knew about him. (When I asked Ian Mackenzie who was a master *sape* player, he recommended Radu.) Last night Varial, who has set up and shot lots of events and concerts in Montreal, recorded a performance by Radu that opened with music by Pharaoh Sanders and a fantastic Moroccan oud player. Radu, who had never gotten such attention, really rose to the occasion. We remind him of British Rajah Brooke, who showed them how to plant cassava. We remind him of the past. "Anytime we see people like you it's like the sun coming out," he says. "You come and teach us things and give us power to protect the forest." Radu appreciates the attention we are trying to bring to their struggle, but also the attention we ourselves give to their forest. Nobody has identified the spectacular profusion of butterflies or beetles at Long Mara'am. I've been telling him about the various families of butterflies and their basic characteristics.

Radu tells me that his ancestor and grandfather, or *tepun*, is the tiger, but the last tiger was killed before he was born. "The tiger makes a trap for all animals," he says. "He puts some very good fruit that animals and humans eat in it and they become food for the tiger. The tiger makes some kind of magic. He knows who will take the fruit so he can attack. We are here because of the magic of our grandfathers.

"Leopard is king now but will not show up for those who do not have knowledge or experience," he goes on. "If you kill the leopard, you are not allowed to bring it back in any way. Must carry and touch first time according to rule. You lift and drop and say I am good and you are the loser. Then prepare rattan basket, put in leopard, and decorate arms and blowgun and head with leaves of *sang* palm. Young leaves, white a little but gold, then you don't bring it straight away to hut, you go and show leaves to the others in camp, so they don't play with the body of leopard and get sick and die. Once the others understand that you have killed leopard, you can bring it back. The one who killed it will skin it and everyone can prepare the carcass and make *atui* log three meters long and both ends like pencil and hit log and dance whole night until next day. Then cook head and take out teeth only for adult people to wear as necklace and in ear hole and skin for dance equipment, put your head in hole over its chest. The skin for dance called *laya*." This is the Sunda clouded leopard of Borneo and Sumatra, *Neofelis diardi*. We are going through the twenty or so animals in Mackenzie's abbreviated Penan dictionary, which Radu has a printout of. Radu only knows *suket* for half a dozen of them.

Long Mara'am, Davie and I agree, is half paradise, half shithole, a constantly shifting kaleidoscope between Westerners' emerald forest/green hell perceptions of the rain forest, a squalid but luminous outpost of Lévi-Strauss's *tristes tropiques*. As in Africa, ineffable beauty can switch to unspeakable horror and back again in the snap of finger. There is no history, no lasting meaning in the tropics. Everything disintegrates, is broken down by a host of detritivores, nothing is preserved. What is no more is soon forgotten in this continuous pageant of rot and renewal.

Davie and I go down to bathe in the river. On the opposite bank a blindingly white egret is pacing with exquisite grace. I can take a picture of it, but the idea that the image of the bird can be captured and preserved is a Western illusion. All there is is the moment. I have known this since I was a boy, and it was reinforced in the sixties by books like Ram Dass's *Be Here Now*, but I have come to accept that I am no good at living in the moment. My mind is too active and disjointed, racing in a million directions, making connections. Cannabis has been a great teacher. It relaxes me and opens me to new dimensions of where I am. As William S. Burroughs put it, in an homage to the plant that he wrote in his eighties for the *New Yorker*, "*quelles conjonctures,*" what connections! But here, sitting on this log with Davie, watching the egret intently picking its way along the opposite shore, my contentment is complete. "This is the life," I tell him, and he says, "It sure is, Panda."

Two years later Davie and I will reminiscence about our trip to Borneo, and in one of his e-mails he will write:

> I was tired of the plight of the Penan to be honest. Probably a very basic trait of my personality, a feeling of ineffectualness and insignificance. And the futility of the common man's struggles with power, money, greed, and progress in general. I felt a bit dishonest because I felt our visit, mine in particular, would not result in any change. They hoped we could do something for them but did they really believe it? I didn't like Christianity's invasion into their culture. What had they bought into, what paper did they sign, with whom did they make an agreement to build that bridge to Long Mara'am? How did they earn the money to buy the motorcycles, etc.? The longhouses, Malaysian projects. And the people lying down for it. Welfare. The little group we stayed with originally, led by that passionate old man, are they representative of some very small, independent groups who have not sold out? Asik evidently still lived the old way. He had no home in that town. I also can't understand people who live without chairs.

Mulu: Forest Primeval

Jimmy comes and we head for Gunung Mulu National Park, which has some of the largest stands of undisturbed Borneo lowland rain forest in Sarawak. We stop for lunch at Long Bedian—with Sagung, who is still there with the girls, and our cook, Edwin, who wants to be an architect but is drunk and ashamed we have found him this way. Then we leave Nelson at his *tana'*, Long Kerong, and spend the rest of the afternoon trying to find the way to Long Iman, our next destination, from which we will take a boat up to the park. We take the wrong road, which is easy, as nothing is marked, and there are dozens of them. At last we find ourselves on the most spectacular knife-edge ridge yet. To the left black eagles and hornbills are coasting below, over a cavernous gorge, then fifty miles of ridge and rain forest sloping down to the converted zone with its millions of oil-palm trees, and Miri and the South China Sea in the hazy distance. To the right, a savanna below with several gumdrop hills of frothing rain forest, shot with a double rainbow. Our destination.

Jimmy lets us out at the end of the ridge. The road has become too steep for his truck. He will meet us here on Thursday at eleven. We take what we will need for the next three days and leave the rest with Jimmy and walk down from the ridge, arriving just after dark at Long Iman, a two-story two-hundred-yard-long megalonghouse with hundreds of Penan, most of them glued to the TV in their extended-family apartments.

In the morning the women are all sitting and kids are playing in the common columned arcade. The women are beading bracelets and weaving things of rattan for the tourists who will come down from Mulu later in the morning, and shelling a delicious black pitted fruit unfamiliar to the three of us, which they give us a taste of.

Jimmy's friend, with whom we crash, plays the *sape*, so we jam for a while, then he runs us up to Mulu in his boat, which takes forty-five minutes. We rent one of the park's comfy bungalows, $120 a night for the three of us, and take a boardwalk out into a flooded forest.

As we stroll on what is billed as the longest canopy walk in the world, 450 meters long, 25 to 30 meters high, dipterocarps tower above: *Shorea, Dipterocarpus, Anisoptera, Dryobalanops, Parashorea, Vatica, Hopea, Cotylelobium, Neobalanocarpus*. These are some of the tallest rain forest trees on Earth. *Tapang* is the tallest and most emergent, its rock-hard, clean white barkless stems writhing up 70 meters. I take a picture of Davie standing between the huge flaring buttresses of a *boenway* tree. Above the forest loom the jagged karst crags of Mount Mulu, which has a suite of vegetation, each with a different set of flora and fauna, up to montane cloud forest.

We finally see a dart-poison tree, *Antiaris toxicaria*. Our previous hosts have been reluctant to take us to their trees, because they are rare and vital to maintaining their proud tradition as blowgun hunters, a tradition all the more important as the authorities make it very difficult for them to get shotguns. They call the poison *ipoh*. While the tree's latex is poisonous, it also serves as a bonding agent for even more potent plant toxins, of which the Penan use about two hundred. Each hunter has his own secret mixture, which he doesn't share even with members of his own band. The word for the tree is *tajem*. According to legend, Tajem was an extremely beautiful and clever woman. Many men fell in love with her. She felt pity for all of them, and thought that if she became close to one of them it would not be fair to the others, so she decided to become something useful for all of them and transformed herself into the tree whose blood they could use for hunting. This tree has been scored many times, by generations of hunters, Penan and another local tribe, the Berawan, who say this is their area. The Penan here are a break-off group from ones in the highlands.

The initial 52,856 hectares of Gunung Mulu National Park were declared a UNESCO World Heritage Site in 1974, and another 28,530 hectares are soon to be added. In 1978 the Royal Geographical Society embarked on a fourteen-month inventory of its flora and fauna. Four hundred and fifty-eight species of ant in seventy-eight genera were identified, more than in all of North America and one of the largest collections ever made in such a small area. Dr. J. D. Holloway was so blown away by the moths that he embarked on his monumental eighteen-volume *Moths of Borneo*, which covers only the 4,500 macromoth species. He also identified 280 butterfly species, and other scientists found 75 frog species; 50 turtles; 25 lizards, geckos, and skinks; 21 colubrids; 3 elapids—cobras and corals; 3 vipers; 65 mammals, including the pig-tailed macaque and two other primates; a flying fox; 16 bat species, including the diadem, round leaf, and horseshoe; and the yellow-throated civet and the banded palm civet. I spend a couple of hours browsing in the massive multivolume report at park headquarters and taking notes.

The Royal Geographical Society expedition discovered Deer Cave, which has the largest subterranean chamber on Earth, five hundred feet wide by three miles deep. We go to visit it late in the day, hoping to witness the mass exodus of the bats. It is four miles from our bungalow. On the way we see red pagoda flowers, a mongoose, a monitor lizard, and the swiftlets from whose nests bird's nest soup is made, a delicacy in Asia. Half the houses in Pangkalanbun had tall wooden boxes with swiftlet holes on their roofs.

The mouth of the cave has *lesai*, or fishtail palms, which have grown to thirty to sixty feet on the limestone and look like giant tree ferns, except that they are bearing fruit. Water dripping from its three-hundred-foot ceiling appears to fall in slow motion. During the daytime, two to three million wrinkle-lipped free-tailed bats, and several million more of two other species, plaster the ceiling. Animals ranging from barking and sambar deer to the gargantuan Rajah Brooke birdwing *Papilio* lick the salts in their guano at the cave's mouth, and at dusk the bats stream out of the cave in long floating ribbons, each of them to consume two-thirds of their body weight, collectively an estimated twenty tonnes of insects a night, and to pollinate durian, eucalyptus, ebony, mahogany, cashew, and a host of other trees. Mulu, the British scientists discovered, was a naturalist's paradise beyond any of their wildest imagining.

Just as the sun is setting, as we are waiting for the bats to fly out of the cave, suddenly, it starts to rain torrentially with no signs of letting up. Rotten luck. They won't be coming out tonight. We dash back to the bungalow and arrive thoroughly soaked.

In 2000 the World Wildlife Fund spearheaded the Heart of Borneo Project, which created a trinational conservation area, comprising five contiguous national parks, including Mulu, one in Brunei (whose rain forest is far more intact because of its prodigious oil reserves), and another in Kalimantan, and the rest—most of the area—a million-hectare buffer zone of protected forest reserves, which can be selectively logged but not cleared or converted and are in various states of degradation, a lot of them having already been logged. So the powers-that-be in Borneo's three national jurisdictions feel that they have done enough to save their forest. "Without [Chief Minister] Taib we'd still be a backwater," Brian Clark, the Australian manager of Gunung Mulu National Park, tells me. "He's developed the state and maintained peace between all the different tribes and races. Every country on Earth has exploited its resources. The West can't condemn any country for it. Canada, USA, and Africa are cutting their forests. It's part of the nature of the beast."

This school of thought—that the destruction of Sarawak's flora and fauna by Taib Inc. is worth the progress it has brought and is "the nature of the beast"—probably has more followers in Sarawak than people who want to save the forest and the indigenous people's cultures and customary land. Even our Penan guide, Israel, an activist Jimmy has instructed to take care of us, tells me, "Taib is the reality. He brought Sarawak into the modern world so he deserves to be paid well, especially because he owns the company."

But Babulu, the seventy-year-old former headman of Bateu Bungan, a half-finished modern Penan village across the Melinau River and upstream a bit from park headquarters, sees things very differently. Babulu is the oldest Penan man we have met. "Money is killing the world," he tells me through his son, the current headman, who is wearing modern clothing, while Babulu has a fantastic feather headdress and a sarong. I concur, "Your words tell the truth of our time," and he continues, "Penan didn't have money in past. They didn't need it. We want to preserve the forest because all the spirits we believe are coming from it. Our elders if they wanted to find God, Balei Pu'un, they went into the forest fasting and singing a special song."

Babulu keeps a one-eyed *olong* pigtail macaque in a cage, who guards the compound and announces visitors, like a watchdog. He is glaring fiercely at us with his one good eye. Babulu's wife, his partner for the last half-century, is plucking a *pagang* zither, a segment of bamboo with raised strings ranged around it. Babulu continues, "My father was witch doctor before Christianity came. He received the knowledge of how to heal sick from his father. When someone is very sick, his soul is almost gone. The witch doctor goes into the forest where there are many spirits, or *balei*, not only Balei Pu'un, but Balei Mungan, and Balei Betala, who created human beings. . . . To call spirit of sick people is just like doctor using stethoscope, and spirit will hear you. The name is called Balei Padeng to make you here, alive again."

"This whole world is sick now," I say. "How can we heal it?"

"Some of the mighty trees in the forest, like *talasci, tano, muteni, gita*, many types of spirit use them as their home. When these trees are cut, it makes the world sick. In the clearing of the village you have many streets, but in the forest you have joy. The solution is not to cut these trees. When you clear the forest, you have stress and sickness. Already many trees have been cut."

Can we bring back the forest?

"We know it's too late, but certain parts of forest we want to be preserved. At least the park is preserved. We really appreciate what the government has done. But this side of the river is being destroyed by logging and we don't want them to continue."

"Why did Balei Pu'un send these people to cut the forest?" I ask, and Babulu says, "When these people were coming in the past to cut the trees a very loud thunderstorm warned them not to destroy our home and many loggers were killed in the forest. This was Balei Pu'un talking, but human beings, they still need to do this."

We continue up the Melinau to Clearwater Cave, whose system is 215.3 kilometers long, the world's longest. It has blind crabs. A Rajah Brooke birdwing, ten inches from black and luminous green wingtip to wingtip, is sucking up the guano salts at its moist mouth with its long unfurled proboscis. We spend three days in this world-class Garden of Eden. There are no big mammals—the last rhino was killed in 1910, and there were never orangutans—but the bird life—120 of Borneo's 420 species—includes green barbets, three models of kingfisher, and eight kinds of hornbill. Twenty-two thousand species of insects, seven thousand of them Lepidoptera (butterflies and moths) and eight thousand of them Coleoptera (beetles) have been identified in the park, and each new entomological expedition finds more.

We take a night walk on the boardwalk with a Penan guide named Susan. The slow loris and western tarsier look like small bug-eyed monkeys, she says. Susan has only seen them once. A small bristly white porcupine-like creature—a moon rat—dashes across the boardwalk right in front of me. Susan shines up with her flashlight a big snail, a luminous green tree frog, a long spiky stick insect. All these things that stay motionless and camouflaged during the day come alive at night.

This completes my tour of the world's great rain forests. Even after spending years exploring those of the Amazon and Equatorial Africa, this one brings home how little I understand of their bewildering diversity.

Bruno and the Battle for the Forest

After three glorious days in Mulu we return to Long Iman and walk up the steep slope to the spectacular ridge where Jimmy is waiting with his truck. We drive downcountry, passing Samling's log pond for the upper Tutoh region. Thousands of fat forty-foot logs of *meranti, kapur, kerning, nyatoh, zupater,* and other valuable hardwoods are waiting to be taken to the sawmill below. The one hundred ringgit the Chinese guy from Melfra Keng is offering each of the Ba Marong to let it destroy their *tana'* is typical, Jimmy says. "The best remuneration any community has negotiated is ten thousand ringgit a year for the length of the operation, three to four years. One hundred ringgit is not even the value of two meters of one of these logs. And they come back four to five times."

Another larger-than-life white guy in Borneo's history, up there with James Brooke and Alfred Russel Wallace, and a major martyr in the battle for the planet, up there with Dian Fossey and Chico Mendes, Bruno Manser is a national hero in Switzerland but virtually unheard of in America. Jimmy is in two films about Manser: the 2001 *Tong Tana*—Manser disappeared two months after its shooting was finished—and a film about the expedition that tried to find him, but there was never a big Hollywood movie about him. Warner Brothers optioned the rights to his life story, and Steven Spielberg was interested, but Manser felt the script took unacceptable liberties with his actual life story, starting with making him an American, and nothing ever came of it, which is why he is still hardly known in the United States. Americans who even know what their consumption of palm oil is doing to Borneo are probably no more than ten thousand, and ones who care enough to get involved even fewer. The number of Westerners who could even find Borneo on a map is not sizeable, and thus the struggles of its people and animals play out in relative obscurity.

Born in Basel in 1954, Manser was an accomplished botanical illustrator. His journals are full of beautiful watercolors of flowers and animals and portraits and sketches of the Penan going about their lives. In 1984 he arrived in Sarawak, part of an expedition that was going to explore the caves of Mulu national park. Wanting to live a life without money and to find "the deep essence of humanity" and "the people who are still living close to their nature," he broke off from the group and bushwhacked alone into the interior of the park, over Mount Mulu and to its eastern side, where he found some still nomadic Penan—Asik Nyelit's group, the Baubung. He lived with them for six years and became one of them—Lakei Penan—and recorded their oral histories in his journals. At this point the deforestation rates in Borneo were dramatic—the highest in recorded history, in fact. Sarawak's chief minister Taib and his family had become extremely rich from timber and oil-palm concessions and sales, well on their way to becoming the billionaires they are today.

Manser, seeing the game being depleted, rivers polluted, the Penans' magical forest world being destroyed, became an activist and the nemesis of Taib. The Penan were a peaceful people. Unlike the other Orang Ulu tribes, they never took heads. In the six years with them Manser claimed he never witnessed any arguments or violence, so he organized peaceful blockades of logging trucks. The first blockade was in 1985. After actions like paragliding down to the front of the chief minister's palace in Kuching with a banner that said *Stop the Logging*, Manser was declared an enemy of state by Taib, who offered a $25,000 reward on his capture, dead or alive. He was captured by soldiers but escaped while being allowed to relieve himself by leaping handcuffed off a bridge into a thundering cataract. In 1990, alerted that he was about to be captured again, he escaped over the Kalimantan border, returned to Switzerland, and for the next ten years devoted himself to rallying international support for the Penan and their forest. As a result of his lectures and more dramatic, Greenpeace-like actions, Al Gore condemned logging activities in Sarawak, Prince Charles called the treatment of the Penan a "genocide," BBC and the National Geographic Channel produced documentaries about the Penan, and the *New Yorker* did a piece on the Penan, Manser, and the logging in 1991.

On July 17 of that year, Manser climbed to the top of a thirty-foot-high lamppost outside the media center of a G-7 summit that was taking place in London and unrolled a banner that contained a message about the plight of Sarawak's rain forest and chained himself to the post for two and a half hours. That year he established a foundation that has since been named the Bruno Manser Fonds (Fund) and has grown to be the most important player in the fight for the Penan and the other Orang Ulu's customary rights and for Sarawak's remaining rain forest.

The Penan Peace Park that it is still working on getting the chief minister's approval for would protect the *tana'* of eighteen Penan communities, 20 percent of the entire forest occupied by Penan. In June 1992
Manser parachuted into a crowded stadium during the Earth Summit
in Rio de Janeiro, Brazil. In December of that year, he led a twenty-day
hunger strike in front of Marubeni Corporation headquarters in To-
kyo, Japan. The following year he went on a sixty-day hunger strike
in front of the Federal Palace of Switzerland (Bundeshaus), which was
supported by thirty-seven organizations and political parties, in an un-
successful attempt to get the Swiss Parliament to ban the importation
of unsustainably harvested tropical timber, but more than a thousand
companies agreed to stop buying it (although the definition and verification of "sustainably harvested" and "not sustainably harvested," and
greenwashing, are serious issues, not only in the tropics). The prime
minister of Malaysia, Mahathir Mohamad, blamed Manser for disrupt-
ing law and order and sent him a letter that said it was "about time that
you stop your arrogance and your intolerable European superiority.
You are no better than the Penan," of whom he said, "It is our policy to
bring all jungle dwellers together into the mainstream. There is nothing
romantic about these helpless, half-starved, and disease-ridden people."
Especially if they are standing in the way of billions worth of timber
and land for oil-palm trees.

But all these actions did little to stop the assault on the forest and the
Penans' world. Taib Inc. was still raking it in, and the rain forest was still
disappearing at a staggering rate. In 2000, deeply discouraged by his
failure to accomplish anything substantive in the developed world or in
Sarawak, he snuck back into Sarawak from Kalimantan, into Bario, a
tourist and trading town on the central ridge. There was still a $25,000
price on his head. He sent a postcard to his girlfriend, Charlotte, in
Switzerland and headed with a thirty-pound pack and a Penan guide
named Paleu for the Bukit Batu Lawi pinnacles, which he had climbed
and which were a spiritual power spot for him and for the local Kelabit
people. They regarded its twin spires, one 2,046 meters, the other 1,850,
as husband and wife protector gods who were the parents of all the
Orang Ulu. The words of a special song, an incantation he had taught
his friends in Basel, had come to him there. Jimmy tells me, "He said
was going to live in a cave with the Pygmies he had met before. Their

cave was near the pinnacle. They were joyful people and sang and made music all the time." But the Penan never heard of such people, and would have known about them, Ian Mackenzie says. "There are dwarves and there is a myth about some little people called *polish* who chop down a giant they think is a strangler fig, but I've never heard of any cave-dwelling Pygmies," and the expedition that tried to find him six months later didn't find any evidence of them, or of him.

Between 1996 and 2000, when he was in Basel, Manser became close friends with Martin Vosseler, whom I met in 2009 while reporting a story about how Switzerland was the greenest country in the world that year, according to the Yale Environmental Index. Vosseler grew up in a high mountain village in the Alps and is a pure soul, dedicated to doing what he can for the embattled natural world and its marginalized and dispossessed indigenous peoples. He sailed the first solar-powered boat across the Atlantic, brought solar-powered electricity and lights to the last community of Carib Indians, on the island of Dominica, walked across America and back, talking to people about global warming, simply trying to find out their positions on the question. "Bruno and I saw each other almost every day over a period of four years," Vosseler told me. "We always started the day with the incantation he composed on the pinnacle. It begins:

Creative force
Who creates life,
Guide us today on our path!
Let our soul wander
On this planet
In love to all creatures.

Bruno told Vosseler that in the beginning he thought the Penans' belief that the trees had spirits, that there were these invisible copies of themselves floating around, and the rest of their multilayered animistic cosmology was so much mumbo jumbo, but one night, alone in the forest toward the end of his six-year stay with the Penan, he slung his hammock over a stream, and its spirit came to him as he was sleeping and terrified the living daylights out of him. Then he realized there was something to their belief system, and started to see the world as they did.

"I took him to the airport when he went back in 2000," Vosseler told me. "He was very down. I think he decided it was a hopeless cause. It was so palpable that I was never going to see him again," he said with a pang of sadness.

When they got in sight of the pinnacles, Manser told Paleu he wanted to continue alone from there. Several search parties of Penan went looking for him in the following weeks. His machete slash marks were tracked to the swamp at the base of the pinnacle. None of the teams dared to climb the sheer last hundred meters of the taller, male pinnacle. Manser could have just stayed up there and checked out and his remains would have been quickly picked apart by black eagles. Or he could have met with foul play from the loggers' thugs or police or soldiers tipped off that he was back.

A new species of goblin spider has been named after him. Vladimir Nabokov wrote that no immortality compares to having your name enshrined in a Latin species name, but these days, the way things are going in Borneo, how long is this goblin spider going to be around?

The Battle for the Dams

We reach Long Lama and cross the Baram river on the ferry with a truck loaded with eighteen tons of palm nuts, the going rate for which is 350 ringgit a ton, so there are $2,100 worth of nuts on the truck, which twenty-two Indonesians spent a day collecting and made a buck apiece, after the food and other supplies they have to buy from the company store for exorbitant prices. It's like slaves picking cotton in the Old South, or the Haitians whose identity papers are taken away and who are put to work on sugar plantations in the Dominican Republic with no way of getting away, or the Malians, many of them children, who work on the cacao plantations of the Ivory Coast so we can have our Mars bars (which contain palm oil, to boot).

The nuts have to be pressed within twenty-four hours and are being taken to a mill down the road. Every four thousand hectares of palm has to have a mill. If this weren't the case, the plantations would be expanding at an even faster rate. Jimmy tells me the big companies have five thousand hectares each, yielding fourteen tons a year.

Across the river, a protest is going on against the Middle Baram Dam, which will flood out twenty thousand Kenyah, Kayan, Iban, and Penan. The government is promising to resettle them, but is not saying where or in what circumstances. Some Penan groups displaced by other dams were resettled on oil-palm estates, where the only livelihood is to join the indentured Indonesians. The 1,500 Western Penan who were logged, burned, and flooded out of their homeland by Bakun Dam have still not been resettled. "The dams are for energy for big companies so they can sell more oil and gas abroad and make more money and for the cement and metal companies who are building them. All for Taib and his family and cronies. Penan and other Orang Ulu will get nothing except diseases from the pollution of their rivers," Jimmy says. Twelve dams are planned by 2020, fifty-two by 2030. Eight are planned in the Baram valley alone, of which this one will be the biggest and most devastating.

"The fifty-two-kilometer road to it is already being built before the environmental impact study has been completed," one of the protestors, a Kayan schoolteacher named Phillip, tells me. They are blocking the entrance to the road, waving placards, chanting native songs. There are only four of them, but "sometimes we get three hundred people," Phillip, who has been manning the protest for two months now, goes on. "The press in Sarawak shuns us like the plague, because they fear the wrath of Taib. You are the first international journalists, or journalists of any kind, we've seen here. Welcome," he says, pouring us some tea. "Our rice paddies have already been flooded by the poorly designed culverts for this road, which are already backed up with debris. Please tell the world what is happening here."

"Bakun, the biggest dam in South Asia, has already been completed and is flooding an area the size of Singapore, displacing ten thousand Orang Ulu who were promised a better life, but they don't have enough land and are suffering unemployment. And now Murum Dam is about to be impounded. It will displace fifteen hundred people. There are big protests at the dam site," he says, which we were hoping to visit, but Jimmy says it is an eight-hour drive, and the police aren't letting anybody through, and we could be arrested if we tried. So we continue down to Miri, where Jimmy takes us to an activist hotel. There we meet more brave Sarawakans who are trying to stop the depredations of Taib Inc. We learn that the organization is laundering illicit profits from its timber and palm-oil operations through one of its many multinational conglomerates: Sakto, which is based in Ottawa, Canada, and run by Taib's oldest daughter, Jamilah, who is married to a Canadian real estate developer named Sean Murray. Sakto has developed some of the most expensive commercial and residential properties in the country's capital. All in all, Taib's siblings, children, and first cousins have a stake in over four hundred companies in twenty-five countries.

Two years later, November 2015, the protest is still going on. Baram Dam, thanks to these efforts, has been put on hold, but the forest that it would flood is still being cut, although the "extra-savage" logging contracts have been canceled, so it's a bittersweet and only partial victory.

Wrap-up in Miri

We are not leaving Sarawak sanguine that the forest or the Penan way of life are going to be saved. Varial shows me a *Newsweek* story someone has e-mailed about the Waorani, the tribe in the Ecuadorian Amazon in one of whose more acculturated and visited and transitional villages, Bameno, he spent three weeks filming his documentary *Contacted*. The story quotes a Capuchin priest who has worked with the Waorani for decades, Miguel Angel Cabodevilla, who describes their cultural disintegration after a recent massacre and revenge massacre by and of uncontacted and contacted members of the tribe as a "hidden tragedy. Today we are tuning in to watch the end of the tribes that have lived thousands of years. They've survived terrible killings, epidemics, plagues, and an incredibly long systematic extermination of their kind that has been going on since the time of conquest. And now, they're being exterminated in our time."

This is happening with the remaining indigenous rain forest people all over the tropics. Survival International, which has Sebastião Salgado as one of its spokesmen and provided intelligence and logistic support for our piece on the Awá, as well as for this visit with the Penan, is the main advocacy group for them.

For Borneo and the Penan, the Bruno Manser Fund is the most important Western advocacy group. Early in 2015, it lodged a formal complaint with the Royal Canadian Mounted Police in Ottawa that documented the laundering of $20 million of corrupt logging proceeds through Sakto. Its executive director, Lukas Straumann, published *Money Logging: On the Trail of the Asian Timber Mafia*, a superb piece of investigative journalism and narrative history that connects the dots and lays out the extent of Taib Inc.'s global holdings. It is full of maps and charts and is the must-have book for anybody who wants to get involved in trying to do something about this environmental and cultural horror show. Wade Davis's blurb reads, "A unique way of life in the rainforests has been destroyed in a single generation. Read this book and weep. But then get angry." Another important source is the online and radio *Sarawak Report*, whose English editor, Claire Rewcastle-Brown, is persona non grata in Malaysia since flying into Kuching and being denied entry in 2013. Brown was recently awarded the Order of the British Empire.

Ian Mackenzie is finishing Galang's autobiography, which will be the definitive ethnography of the Penan and at four volumes promises to be a magisterial, monumental celebration and documentation of their belief system and way of life. When I talked to him in the fall of 2015, he had just got back from visiting Galang and said it was "business as usual" in Sarawak. Taib, now eighty-five, has stepped down as chief minister and is now the governor of Sarawak, a traditionally ceremonial position, from which he is still running the show. "The Straumann book has caused some consternation in Malaysia, where it is selling well," Mackenzie said. "There has been a cosmetic crackdown on small-time loggers and palm growers, but not of the big guys, who are being a little more careful. Its revelations are extremely embarrassing to Taib and his family and cronies, but there have been no lawsuits because the information in it is sound and meticulously documented."

Giving me and Davie big hugs, Varial returns to Kota Kinabalu with his powerful images and video footage and flies from there to Paris for Christmas with his family. We are still trying to find a network to take on our show, *Suitcase on the Loose*, whose mission is to get the word out about vanishing Edens like the Borneo rain forest to people who don't read books or ten-thousand-word pieces anymore. Still, DispatchesFromTheVanishingWorld.com, the website my son Andre and I launched in 2001, gets almost ten thousand unique visitors from ninety-some countries a month. I just (on February 16, 2015) posted Dispatch #95, *Smithsonian Magazine*'s distillation of this text, "In Borneo's Ruined Forest, Nomads Have Nowhere to Go," with Varial's powerful photos. Judging from the e-mails it has elicited, and the comments on my numerous Facebook posts, Americans are beginning to get the message about the far-off devastating impacts of their consumption of palm oil.

Davie and I fly back up to Kuala Lumpur and hug and head off to our separate connections. "That was the trip of a lifetime, Panda," he tells me.

"It sure was, Davie. The trip our whole lives were preparing us for, and I have a feeling it won't be the last."

"Well, you know where to reach me," he says. "Just give me a shout, and I'll be on the next plane."

As I sit on the plane to Dubai, I feel so happy to have reconnected with Davie, my best childhood buddy. Even though we were different then and still are, I know now that we will be friends again.

The Latest on the Battle for Borneo

On a promising, guardedly positive note, Unilever, Nestlé, and Kraft, three of the biggest buyers of palm oil, have recently canceled contracts with suppliers whose oil-palm-growing practices were deemed unsustainable, and a fourth, Cargill, has marked the anniversary of its no-deforestation pledge with a new forest policy. In addition, toy makers Hasbro, Mattel, and Lego have pledged not to buy their packaging with unsustainable Asia Pulp and Paper, and KFC, Taco Bell, and Pizza Hut have adopted a "zero-deforestation policy for palm oil." Progress is being made as pressure is put on by the consumers and by activist groups like Greenpeace, the Union of Concerned Scientists, and Say No to Palm Oil, but it continues to be undermined by the corruption of local government and contractors, and "zero deforestation" may still include selective logging. And the "sustainable" silviculture the growers claim to be doing, like leaving a band of forest along the watercourses and thin corridors for orangutans and pygmy elephants, doesn't really work. Plus verification of even these half measures is a big problem.

The latest bad actor to make the bad actors list is PepsiCo, which consumes 447,000 tonnes of "conflict" (i.e., not "sustainable" or "sustainable-yield") palm oil a year. Doritos is saturated with it. The damage control flacks at the American multinational food, snack, and beverage corporation say, "PepsiCo has repeatedly stated that we are absolutely committed to 100 percent sustainable palm oil in 2015 and to zero deforestation in our activities and sourcing," but Rainforest Action Network and SumOfUs, a worldwide movement of over 5.4 million consumers, workers, and investors working to hold corporations accountable, find no evidence that it is doing either.

There have been some encouraging macrostudies of late: one finds that there are seven times more trees growing on the planet than previously estimated, and this could be an underestimate. Great news for carbon sequestration. But we are still cutting fifteen billion trees a year and there are only half as many as there were at the end of the last ice age. And in the Amazon, another less encouraging study finds that the approximately three billion trees there now are absorbing one-third less atmospheric carbon than the trees there were thirty years ago. This is because many of the trees have reached the saturation point in terms of how much carbon they can store, while others, experiencing a dramatic growth spurt from all the CO_2 we are pouring into the atmosphere, are dying more quickly. Plus there were two killer droughts in the Amazon Valley, in 2005 and 2010, because of an El Niño–like warming event in the tropical North Atlantic that is happening with increasing frequency and severity due to global warming. The Amazon is often described as "the lung of the world" because it produces so much of our atmospheric oxygen—25 percent of the terrestrial production. But this is not as much as the boreal forest of North America and Siberia, while the main oxygen producers are the phytoplankton on the surface of the world's oceans.

Another morale-building new study, by the UN's Food and Agriculture Organization (FAO), reports that the rate of deforestation in tropical forests worldwide has decreased by 50 percent since 1975. But let's not get too excited: the deforestation rate forty years ago was the highest in human history, particularly on Borneo. And how much of this new, encouraging finding is an artifact of things like "sustainable" oil-palm plantations not being counted in the deforested tally? On the ground, this FAO metastudy is little consolation for the orangutans and the other denizens of Indonesia's remaining rain forest, who at the end of 2015 were fleeing the flames and gagging on the smoke of the worst peat forest fires since 1997. They were so bad the smoke was visible from space (in photos from NASA), and Indonesia's president had to ask for international assistance in putting them out.

Some of the burning peat forest was in Rimba Raya, where I had dinner with Dr. Galdikas and the beautifully mannered orangutan Kristin, who, she told me, was found dead in her nest in 2014, apparently from snakebite. Rimba Raya was in the part of primeval forest that she was hoping to release more of the orangutans from her care center into. But that was granted to an oil-palm company by the third minister of forestry since the pioneering REDD project at Rimba Raya got going. The project is still alive, but when I talked to Dr. B at the beginning of 2016, she had just come back from Kalimantan and was exhausted and distraught: "We have released sixty or so orangutans, most of them in Rimba Raya, and still have two hundred and thirty orangutans at our care center, and now we are getting terribly emaciated ones that have been rescued from the out-of-control peat fires all over Kalimantan, and are trying to bring them back to health. The situation for the orangutans, and the people, is as dire as I've ever seen it. My husband [a local Dayak] was hospitalized for a week for smoke inhalation after fighting the fires on the front line for a month, and I had such a bad cough from all the smoke around our house, which is next to the care center, that it could be heard through three rooms, and finally became really painful. Even in downtown Pangkalanbun you can hardly breathe.

"If REDD hadn't come in," she continued, "all of Rimba Raya would be gone, so I'm really grateful to them. We're trying to put together a corridor of forest for our rescued and rehabilitated orangutans south of the care center, before it's logged and burned and converted to oil palm. But the price for an acre of forest has gone up from one hundred dollars an acre to five hundred dollars, and now we have to get more fruit and medicine for the orangutans that are coming in, and the price of durian fruit, their favorite food, has also shot up. With no forest to feed them, more wild orangutans are raiding local people's settlements and gardens and are often being killed in a brutal way. What they are going through, not only the sheer horror of seeing their forest world go up in smoke, but starving to death and being killed by the local people, is unimaginable."

So this is not the time to let ourselves be lulled into a sense of complacency, about Borneo or anywhere else in the world, much as the carbon capitalists and global warming deniers would like us to be.

Lukas Straumann, executive director of the Bruno Manser Fund, is the new nemesis of Taib Inc. The publication of his book *Money Logging* in 2014 has been a major embarrassment, with its unassailably documented exposés of what has been going on in Sarawak and all over the world. Straumann is a very different kettle of fish from Manser, and brings to rain forest and indigenous-people activism a seldom-seen set of skills. "My background is as a historian, environmental and business," he told me. "My first job was with a Swiss government commission looking into Swiss wartime involvement with the Nazis." Straumann has headed the BMF since 2004. "I never met Bruno, though I studied in Basel a few hundred meters from BMF's office," he goes on. "I knew him as a public figure, of course. When I took over his office it had been four years since his disappearance, but no one had cleared up his office because they were expecting him to come back. I don't think he was killed. By then, 2000, he was no longer a threat to Taib, just a nuisance. A helicopter searched the top of the pinnacle a year after he disappeared, but there was nothing. But he could have been eaten by eagles by then. In support of the suicide theory, he did make out a will and send postcards from Bario before he set out into the forest. I think he could have had an accident, alone in the forest with a big pack. But nothing has been found."

Last year Straumann tried to get Taib's daughter, Jamilah, and her Canadian husband, Sean Murray, prosecuted for laundering $25 million of her dad's illegal timber profits in their real estate development company, Sakto, which has built some of the most expensive commercial and residential buildings in Ottawa. "The Royal Canadian Mounted

Police has been dragging its heels for three years," he said, "so I am flying to Ottawa to meet with the OECD [Organisation for Economic Co-operation and Development] to see if it can prosecute them." The next day, I got this press release from the Bruno Manser Fund in Basel:

15 January 2016

BMF invokes OECD rules against Taib family's secret international holdings

The Bruno Manser Fund requests the disclosure of a Malaysian political family's global assets—Canada's Sakto Group accused of breaching OECD disclosure standards for multinational enterprises.

During our Skype, Straumann made an important point I wasn't aware of: the trade agreement of the Trans-Pacific Partnership will remove the duties on Malaysian palm oil (don't know about Indonesia), so there will be a lot more demand for it in the United States, with free trade making it cheaper. Switzerland has a 100 percent duty on it. Nestlé says it has to be sustainable, but Lukas agrees with Ian Mackenzie that the whole concept of sustainable palm oil is essentially bullshit. You leave a corridor of rain forest for the orangutans and other animals and a little strip on the waterways and plant the rest with oil palm. But you've wiped out the forest. How is that sustainable?

The latest from Lukas is that the BMF has filed suit with the Australian government demanding that it freeze the millions of assets that Taib Inc. has in Australian real estate, like the Adelaide Hilton; a Senate inquiry has been launched. Also, the *Sarawak Report* has discovered that the Yaw family, the owner of the Samling timber group, has been laundering the proceeds of illegal and corrupt logging and oil-palm conversion in Sarawak through an American real estate development company called Sunchase, which has been building major master-planned communities in northern California and the Arizona desert, such as Mountain House, Estrella, and Lincoln Crossing.

In March came unbelievable, miraculous news: Sarawak's new chief minister, Adenan Satem, has officially scrapped Baram Dam. All logging of the area to be flooded has stopped, and twenty thousand Orang

Ulu will not be displaced but will have their land returned to them. Whether the government bowed to the protests or the growing international pressure, or Satem is trying to distance himself from his predecessor, or to regain the trust of rural communities ahead of a crucial state election, is the subject of feverish speculation in Kuching and by Borneo watchers abroad. The cancellation of the Baram Dam plans is expected to trigger a review of all megadam projects in Sarawak.

And more good news from "Jimmy Parang," whom I had e-mailed because my copy editor couldn't find any logging company called Melfra Keng operating in Sarawak, nor could Lukas Straumann. He replied on June 7:

> Hi Alex,
>
> Thanks for your e-mail. Your article was given to me by a University researcher and it was great to read it. The name "Melfra Keng" is what is only known by the local communities where they operate. As you know some of the logging contractors purposely hide their company's name from the community because they know that their activities sometimes illegal. I do hear of the name Mafera and GT but I'm not sure which one is working in Ba Marong area.
>
> I went to Ba Marong last week and they told me that the company has pulled out last year after they were being resisted/disallowed by the Ba Marong community. I spend three days helping the community to plant rubber and local species of trees and they were very happy to have them planted into polybags which they will transfer to the field in six months' time. Now they have a permanent house sponsored by some friends around and also clean gravity water pipe. They have moved further inside where there is pristine forest around their village.

So things are starting to happen, at the final hour. A wave of revulsion against the impacts of palm oil and logging in Borneo and the rest of Southeast Asia seems to be building in the zeitgeist, as more and more people realize what is happening. We have to keep the pressure on.

My latest writing efforts are on behalf of the giraffes, whose numbers have plummeted from something like one hundred and forty thousand to ninety thousand in the last fifteen years. It has been called a "silent extinction" because nobody knows about it or is talking about it, any more than they are aware of or care about what palm oil is doing to the biocultural diversity of Borneo. So I'm writing a piece about it for *Smithsonian Magazine*, for which I spent three weeks in Uganda's Murchison Falls National Park with the incomparable wildlife photographer Melissa Groo. We saw and hung out with more than a thousand Rothschild's giraffes, as well as lions, elephants, zebras, hippos, waterbuck, bushbuck, impalas, kobs, hartebeest, warthogs, and hundreds of species of birds. Never have I experienced the primordial pageant of life and death on the African savanna as I did on this safari. Melissa and I both agreed that what happens when you are looking at an animal, really taking in the perfection of its body and movements, you *become* it, you lose yourself in it, and this activation of your biophilia and your sense of kinship with life produces a euphoria, same as if you are taking in and interacting with, and flashing heavily on a beautiful member of your own species to whom you are very attracted. And when you lose yourself completely, in both cases, becoming an animal or one with your romantic partner, this is love. You have to give yourself totally, shut down the internal monologue, put down the camera and the notebook, and settle into the time and space of the animal or animals or indigenous people you don't have a word in common with. And there's always an element of risk when you give yourself or lose yourself completely. But that's what has to happen, in true love. You have to let yourself go.

It's as simple as that. I wish more people could have the experiences I have been so blessed to have. Then they would understand what we are losing, and what only a collective change of heart, and some persuasive activism to get it going, can maybe save.

I for one have become more conscious of my palm-oil consumption and have gotten it down to a tiny squib of toothpaste twice a day, a shower and shampoo a couple of times a week, not every day, and instead of peanut butter I'm eating roasted peanuts in their shells. Not that this is going to do much for the rape of Borneo, but at least I'm doing something. What I hope is that my readers will want to put their feet down and say no to palm oil, to urge anyone who cares about our world, about the people and animals who inhabit it, to wake up to what's happening in Borneo, and all over the forests and natural habitats of the Earth, to get involved, so maybe this thing can be turned around. The scrapping of Baram Dam has shown what peaceful mass protests that are not going to go away can do, as did the demonstration in front of the White House that got the Keystone Pipeline vetoed. Now it's time to do our part at the consumer end. And an alternative to palm oil must be found so this holocaust ends.

ACKNOWLEDGMENTS

THIS BOOK HAS TRULY BEEN a collaborative effort. First and foremost, it would never have seen the light of day without Alexis Rizzuto, who is not only a superb editor but a devoted animal lover who has dedicated much of her career to editing books that make people care about our embattled fellow sentient beings, in the hope that some of them will join the struggle to keep our wild brothers and sisters with us and to keep what is left of their wild habitat from being destroyed. Alexis got my attention when she was the only editor in a dozen of the most distinguished houses who wanted to do a book about elephants and ivory poaching based on my 2012 *Vanity Fair* piece, "Agony and Ivory." The proposal was submitted before the article was published, and all the other editors said dismaying things like, I'm on the same page with you, but I'm afraid I must pass. But Alexis pleaded passionately to do this book with me. Then the piece went unexpectedly viral and played a major role in igniting the ongoing global campaign to stop the slaughter of Africa's elephants and the consumption of their ivory, mainly by the Chinese. I didn't resubmit the book to the editors who had said no, and I didn't do the book with Alexis, either, having moved on to other pressing projects. But when the idea of doing this book started to take shape, I immediately sent the proposal to Alexis, and we were on. Alexis really went the extra mile, cut me no slack when I blathered on too long, or people needed more characterization, or more information was needed, or a clearer narrative through-line needed to be drawn. I thought I would be in and out of this book in three months, but we ended up spending more than a year on it. Alexis insisted that it, my eleventh book and first one in twenty years, be as good as it could possibly be. I learned a lot about my own craft in the process, which I thought I had down after practicing it for fifty years. So this book is as much Alexis's as it is Alex's. And our text was then read through by Beacon's director, Helene Atwan, and Melissa Nasson, who had further suggestions that were all on the mark. To call the final product a collaboration is an understatement.

If Dr. Biruté Mary Galdikas had not given me so much of her precious time in Kalimantan, I would not have become aware of the horrors Borneo's orangutans are suffering, or of the ravages that the logging and palm oil are doing to the world's oldest and most species-rich forest. And if Ian Mackenzie had not given me a week of his life, at least, to make sure I got the section on the Penan as right as I could, it wouldn't have anything like the accuracy it does. Survival International connected me with our activist guide, "Jimmy Parang," who organized our three-week reporting and photo safari in Sarawak and made sure we met the people we needed to meet and saw the things we needed to see.

David Holderness was not only a joy to be reunited with after fifty-five years but a great sounding board for my impressions. My brother, Nick, and my late father, Nick, inspired me with a love of the natural world that has been the driving force of my writing career, and like so many others have been supportive and key role models and have opened my eyes to what is going on. Any impact this book may have on its readers is as much due to their input as it is to mine. I cannot thank you all enough!

NOTES

FOR A LIST OF PRODUCTS containing palm oil that ranks them "sustainable yield" or not (which I am not going to endorse or dispute, the whole notion of sustainable palm oil being questionable), please go to www.beacon.org/borneo.

page 4: *the deforestation rate in Borneo* . . . See Tina Butler, "Deforestation in Borneo," *Mongabay*, April 13, 2005, http://news.mongabay.com/2005/04 /deforestation-in-borneo.

page 5: *two gutsy investigators with Global Witness* . . . See "Inside Malaysia's Shadow State," YouTube video, posted by Global Witness, March 18, 2013, https://www.youtube.com/watch?v=_1RRNggnM6A.

page 5: *"It's in everything now"* . . . A long list of products containing palm oil can be found on http://www.beacon.org/borneo.

page 9: *"A large part of our attitude"* . . . Albert Einstein, "The Negro Question," 1946.

page 14: *Paul Shepard writes* . . . Paul Shepard, *Nature and Madness* (San Francisco: Sierra Club Books, 1982).

page 34: *"sacrificing their future"* . . . Alison Jolly, *Madagascar* (Oxford, UK: Pergamon Press, 1984).

page 34: *"this insular sub-region"* . . . Alfred Russel Wallace, "The Fauna of Madagascar and the Mascarene Islands," *Madagascar Magazine* 10 (December 1886).

page 36: *dogs getting excited* . . . See Rupert Sheldrake, *Dogs That Know When Their Owners Are Coming Home: And Other Unexplained Powers of Animals* (New York: Crown, 1999).

page 36: *"whiffs of the uncanny"* . . . I have had these moments of heightened consciousness and connectedness in all sorts of circumstances, such as canoeing the Bloodvein River in Manitoba, for instance. See the beginning and end of "Dispatch #28: Manitoba's Many-Headed Hydro," *Dispatches from the Vanishing World* (blog), June 9, 2005, http://blog.dispatchesfrom thevanishingworld.com/dispatch-27-who-owns-this-river/, or people watching at the window of the Red Flame Diner in midtown Manhattan; see the end of "Dispatch #78: Positively 44th Street," *Dispatches from the Vanishing World* (blog), June 19, 2012, originally published in *Vanity Fair*, May 18, 2012, http://www.vanityfair.com/style/2012/06/new-york-city -manhattan-west-44th-street-harvard-club-new-yorker-algonquin.

page 59: *"strik[ing] back at a natural world"* . . . Shepard, *Nature and Madness*, 124.

page 59: *"nature-deficit disorder"* . . . Richard Louv, *Last Child in the Woods: Saving Our Children from Nature-Deficit Disorder* (Chapel Hill, NC: Algonquin Books, 2005).

page 59: *solastalgia* . . . Daniel B. Smith, "Is There an Ecological Unconscious," *New York Times Magazine*, January 27, 2010. The term "ecological unconscious" was coined by Theodore Roszak.

page 64: *"a Kama Sutra of erotic possibility"* . . . Dale Peterson, *The Moral Lives of Animals* (New York: Bloomsbury, 2012), 135.

Page 69: *lessens the gap* . . . See Laurel Braitman's book about her work as an animal psychologist, *Animal Madness: How Anxious Dogs, Compulsive Parrots, and Elephants in Recovery Help Us Understand Ourselves* (New York: Simon & Schuster, 2014).

Page 69: *"a bunch of emotionally disturbed kids"* . . . Temple Grandin, *Animals in Translation: Using the Mysteries of Autism to Decode Animal Behavior* (New York: Scribner Classics, 2010).

page 73: *a cockatoo named Snowball* . . . Aniruddh D. Patel et al., "Investigating the Human-Specificity of Synchronization to Music," in *Proceedings of the 10th International Conference on Music Perception and Cognition*, ed. Mayumi Adachi et al. (Sapporo, Japan: ICMPC, 2008), CD-ROM.

page 73: *As Roy Scranton writes* . . . In *Learning to Die in the Anthropocene: Reflections on the End of a Civilization* (San Francisco: City Lights Books, 2015), 55.

page 82: *probably what got her killed* . . . After my 1986 piece about Fossey's murder, a new suspect, considered by many to be the most likely, emerged: the governor of the prefecture of Ruhengeri, Protais Zigiranyirazo, commonly known as Monsieur Zed ("Mr. Z"). His brother-in-law was President Juvénal Habyarimana, whose plane was shot down on April 7, 1994, triggering the Rwandan genocide. Apparently Fossey found out Zigiranyirazo was selling baby gorillas to zoos in Europe, which required wiping out their entire families, and she went ballistic and stormed into his office and gave him bloody murder in front of his staff, which was not done, especially by a woman, and he had her killed. But Zed was never charged, and was acquitted on other charges of participating in the genocide, and is now living in Abidjan on the Ivory Coast.

page 84: *They treat each other with plants* . . . See Matt Walker, "Wild Orangutans Treat Pain with Natural Anti-Inflammatory," *New Scientist*, July 28, 2008, https://www.newscientist.com/article/dn14406-wild-orangutans-treat-pain-with-natural-anti-inflammatory.

page 90: *they've taken to the marvelous gadgets* . . . See Katherine Fernandez-Blance, "Toronto Zoo Orangutans Go Ape for iPad," *Toronto Star*, December 26, 2012, http://www.thestar.com/news/gta/2012/08/23/toronto_zoo_orangutans_go_ape_for_ipad.html.

page 91: *In 2004 we started a roundtable* . . . See "The Oil Palm," Forum for Sustainable Palm Oil, http://www.forumpalmoel.org/en/ueber-palmoel.html; and "Palm Oil," Say No to Palm Oil, http://www.saynotopalmoil.com/Whats_the_issue.php.

page 95: *"The welcoming committee"* . . . Alex Shoumatoff, "The Last of Eden," *Vanity Fair*, December 2013.

page 99: *"I realized that the Penans"* . . . Ian prefers to add an *s* when referring to more than one Penan, like *Navajos* instead of *Navajo*.

page 100: *is devoting himself to documenting indigenous people* . . . See his website, http://varialstudio.com.

page 100: *our multiplatform docuseries* . . . For the proposal and teaser, see "*Suitcase on the Loose*—Trailer—Borneo: The Last Penan Hunter-Gatherers," Vimeo video, posted by Varial Cédric Houin, January 23, 2014, http://www.vimeoinfo.com/video/84895798/suitcase-on-the-loose-trailer-borneo-the.

page 101: *"committed to implementing sustainable forest management practices"* . . . "Upstream Timber Operations," Samling.com, 2016.

page 104: *We head out of Miri* . . . The best map of the Penan homeland, with the communities we visited, is on the Bruno Manser Fonds' website: http://www.bmf.ch/en/documentation/sarawak-geoportal.

page 106: *Its tree species per hectare count* . . . See James LaFrankie, "Initial Findings from Lambir: Trees, Soils and Community Dynamics," Center for Tropical Forest Science 5 (1995); and "Yasuni," Center for Tropical Forest Science, Smithsonian Tropical Research Institute, http://www.ctfs.si.edu/site/4.

page 106: *the most species-rich on Earth* . . . See Marco C. Roos et al., "Species Diversity and Endemism of Five Major Malesian Islands: Diversity-Area Relationships," *Journal of Biogeography* 31 (2004): 1893–1908.

page 107: *One tree can produce four million flowers* . . . See "Borneo," Mongabay, http://pt.mongabay.com/borneo.html.

page 109: *"a commodified landscape"* . . . J. Peter Brosius, "Between Development and Deforestation: Negotiating Citizenship in a Commodified Landscape," *Akademika* 42 & 43, no. 1 (1993): 87–194.

page 111: *the Great Cave of Niah* . . . See "Niah National Park," Sarawak Forestry Corporation, http://www.sarawakforestry.com/htm/snp-np-niah.html.

page 113: *adaptation to new ecological circumstances* . . . A similar process took place in the sixteenth century in the Amazon, when the Portuguese arrived and started to enslave the people on the main river, who had thriving plantations and river-turtle farms, and the ones who escaped fled up to the headwaters of its tributaries and became hunter-gatherers. This, too, was described as cultural devolution, but is now seen as adaptation, one of the many examples of cultural fluidity in our collective past.

page 116: *"ecologically noble savage"*. . . In "The Ecologically Noble Savage," *Orion* 9 (1990): 24–29.

page 120: *a new report* . . . Penan Support Group, *A Wider Context of Sexual Exploitation of Penan Women and Girls in Middle and Ulu Baram, Sarawak, Malaysia* (Selangor, Malaysia: SUARAM Kommunikasi, 2013).

page 123: empates, *to stop the ranchers* . . . See "Dispatch #012: Murder in Brazil, the Rain-Forest Martyr Chico Mendes," *Dispatches from the Vanishing World* (blog), November 14, 2012, http://blog.dispatchesfromthevanishingworld.com/murder-in-brazil-the-rain-forest-martyr-chico-mendes/, originally published in *Vanity Fair*, April 1989.

page 127: *"nature is pure and noble"* . . . Biruté M. F. Galdikas, *Reflections of Eden: My Years with the Orangutans of Borneo* (New York: Little, Brown, 1995).

page 127: *This world, middle-earth* . . . See Hans Schareer, *Ngaju Religion: The Conception of God Among a South Borneo People*, trans. Rodney Needham (The Hague: Martinus Nijhoff, 1963).

page 134: *has a great book called* . . . Stephen Corry, *Tribal Peoples for Tomorrow's World* (Alcester, SD: Freeman Press, 2011).

page 152: *There are no true nomads* . . . A one-hour documentary, *The Last Nomads*, about Mackenzie's work and the destruction of the forest and the end of the Penans' nomadic way of life, was produced by the linguistic anthropologist Andrew Gregg in 2008.

page 154: *Mackenzie's abbreviated Penan dictionary* . . . The entire lexicon is downloadable from Ian Mackenzie's website: http://www.rimba.com/pdindexf/pdindex.html.

page 161: *"deep essence of humanity"* . . . *Encyclopedia of Religion and Nature*, ed. Bron Taylor, vol. 1, *A–J* (London: Continuum, 2008), 1046–47.

page 162: *recorded their oral histories in his journals* . . . Manser published *Voices from the Rainforest: Testimonies of a Threatened People* (Selangor, Malaysia: Bruno Manser Foundation and INSAN, 1996) a year after starting a foundation now called the Bruno Manser Fonds after him. It drew on his notebooks, ten thousand photographs, illustrations, and recordings of Penans' oral history. The actual notebooks were published in full in Ruedi Suter, *Rainforest Hero: The Life and Death of Bruno Manser* (Basel: Bergli Books, 2015). Lukas Straumann's *Money Logging: On the Trail of Asia's Timber Mafia* (Basel: Bergli Books 2014) has several chapters on Manser's life and career.

page 163: *"It is our policy"* . . . Simon Elegant, "Without a Trace," *Time*, September 3, 2001.

page 167: *"extra-savage" logging* . . . Lukas Straumann, personal communication.

page 167: *a bittersweet and only partial victory* . . . Rod Harbinson, "Indigenous Activists Celebrate Bitter Victory over Rainforest Dam Moratorium," *Ecologist*, October 22, 2015, http://www.theecologist.org/campaigning/2985977/indigenous_activists_celebrate_bitter_victory_over_rainforest_dam_moratorium.html.

page 169: *a new forest policy* . . . Cargill, "Cargill Marks Anniversary of No-Deforestation Pledge with New Forest Policy," news release, September 17, 2015, http://www.cargill.com/news/releases/2015/NA31891862.jsp.

page 169: *"zero-deforestation policy for palm oil"* . . . See Pablo Pacheco, "Zero Deforestation in Indonesia: Pledges, Politics, and Palm Oil," *Forest News* (blog), January 7, 2016, http://blog.cifor.org/39085/zero-deforestation-in-indonesia-pledges-politics-and-palm-oil?fnl=en.

page 170: *the latest bad actor* . . . Jennifer Elks, "PepsiCo Reacts to New Ads Slamming Doritos over Lax Palm Oil Policy," *Sustainable Brands*, January 16, 2015, http://www.sustainablebrands.com/news_and_views/behavior_change/jennifer_elks/pepsico_reacts_new_ads_slamming_doritos_over_lax_palm_o.

page 170: *and this could be an underestimate* . . . Tim Radford, "Global Tree Census Highlights Need to Restore Forests," Climate News Network, September 4, 2015, http://climatenewsnetwork.net/global-tree-census-highlights-need-to-restore-forests.

page 170: *approximately three billion trees* . . . Robert McSweeney, "Amazon Rainforest Is Taking Up a Third Less Carbon Than a Decade Ago," *CarbonBrief*, March 18, 2015, http://www.carbonbrief.org/amazon-rainforest-is-taking-up-a-third-less-carbon-than-a-decade-ago.

page 170: *an El Niño–like warming event* . . . See my story, "Dispatch #41: The Dehydration of the Amazon Rainforest," *Dispatches from the Vanishing World*

(blog), August 9, 2007, part 1, http://www.dispatchesfromthevanishing
world.com/dispatch39/05AMAZONmech1.pdf and part 2, http://www
.dispatchesfromthevanishingworld.com/dispatch39/05AMAZONmech2
.pdf, originally published as "The Gasping Forest," *Vanity Fair*, May 2007.

page 170: *the rate of deforestation in tropical forests worldwide* . . . Max Green,
"FAO Finds Positives in New Deforestation Report," Agra Europe, September 7, 2015, https://www.agra-net.com/agra/agra-europe/policy-and
-legislation/environment/fao-finds-positives-in-new-deforestation-report
-490536.htm.

page 171: *let's not get too excited* . . . This stomach-turning series of maps shows
the progression: "Graph of the Day: Observed and Projected Deforestation
in Borneo, 1950–2020," *Desdemona Despair*, July 7, 2010, http://www
.desdemonadespair.net/2010/07/graph-of-day-observed-and-projected.html.

page 171: *ask for international assistance* . . . Ben Bland, "Forest Fire Risk for
Indonesia's Orangutans," BBC, October 10, 2015, http://www.bbc.com
/news/world-asia-34494904.

page 171: *The project is still alive* . . . To keep abreast of developments, see
https://orangutan.org, the website of Orangutan Foundation International, which Dr. Galdikas founded in 1986.

page 171: *as dire as I've ever seen it* . . . See Orangutan Foundation International's annual report for 2015 at https://orangutan.org/about/annual
-report/.

page 173: *the Yaw family* . . . "Found! Sarawak's Stolen Wealth Is Locked in
a Treasure Trove in the United States!," *Sarawak Report*, April 25, 2016,
http://www.sarawakreport.org/2016/04/found-sarawaks-stolen-wealth-is
-locked-in-a-treasure-trove-in-the-southern-united-states/.

page 174: *"Your article was given to me"* . . . See Alex Shoumatoff, "The Lost
World," *Smithsonian*, March 2016, http://www.smithsonianmag.com
/science-nature/borneos-ruined-forests-nomads-have-nowhere-to-go
-180958107/.

page 175: *wildlife photographer Melissa Groo* . . . This was our third collaboration, after the sandhill cranes of Nebraska and the white spirit bear of
British Columbia, both on my website: http://blog.dispatchesfromthe
vanishingworld.com.